31
Days of
Prayer

31 Days of Prayer

Moving God's Mighty Hand

Ruth Myers

and

Warren Myers

Multnomah Books

31 DAYS OF PRAYER

© 1997 by Warren and Ruth Myers
International Standard Book Number: 978-1-60142-316-0

Cover image by Photodisc

Unless otherwise indicated, Scripture quotations are from:
New American Standard Bible © 1960, 1977 by the Lockman Foundation
Other Scripture quotations:
The Holy Bible, New International Version (NIV) © 1973, 1984 by International
Bible Society, used by permission of Zondervan Publishing House *The Holy Bible,*
New King James Version (NKJV) © 1984 by Thomas Nelson, Inc. *The Holy Bible,*
King James Version (KJV) *Holy Bible,* New Living Translation (NLT) © 1996. Used
by permission of Tyndale House Publishers, Inc. All rights reserved. *The Holy Bible,*
New Century Version (NCV) © 1987, 1988, 1991 by Word Publishing Used by
permission. *The New Testament in Modern English, Revised Edition* (Phillips) © 1958,
1960, 1972 by J. B. Phillips *The Amplified Bible* (AMP) © 1965, 1987 by Zondervan
Publishing House. *The Amplified New Testament* ® 1958, 1987 by the Lockman
Foundation. *The New Testament: An Expanded Translation* Kenneth S. Weust (Weust)
copyright © 1961 by Wm. B. Eerdmans

Published in the United States by Multnomah, an imprint of the Crown
Publishing Group, a division of Penguin Random House LLC, New York.

MULTNOMAH® and its mountain colophon are registered trademarks of Penguin
Random House LLC.

Printed in the United States of America

2020
20 19 18 17 16 15 14 13 12 11 10

This book made available without charge by The 1687 Foundation, a nonprofit,
tax-exempt organization dedicated to advancing Christian and charitable
purposes. Please note that this book may only be given away as a free gift. It may
not be sold, used as an encouragement for any charitable gifts, or provided for any
commercial or personal-gain purpose whatsoever.

For additional information, please contact:
www.1687foundation.com
Tel: 541.549.7600
Fax: 541.549.7603

Contents

FOREWORD

During a time of illness and severe testing for my first wife, Billie, and me, a dear friend sent us a book of praises. *31 Days of Praise* by Ruth Myers turned out to be a gracious gift from the Lord. As we prayed together through the daily praises, our spirits were lifted into the presence of our loving, caring God. Time and again, we found ourselves refreshed and strengthened. We saw God's hand at work in many ways we might have missed.

I've been blessed by many inspirational books throughout my fifty-two years of ministry around the world with Billy Graham. But in the months before my wife Billie's homegoing in 1994, those praise-filled prayers were one of God's most memorable kindnesses to us. I've been recommending *31 Days of Praise* to friends ever since.

I believe the book that you are now holding, by Ruth and her husband, Warren, has been touched by God for the same type of ministry. *31 Days of Prayer* is meant for you if you want to become more effective and fulfilled in your praying. It's for you if you long, as I do, to know God better, to treasure in your heart and life what He treasures.

In God's mercy and extravagant grace, He has recently brought Ann Prince into my life to be my wife. As we read the manuscript together, we both remarked what a tremendous source of help and encouragement the Myerses' new book will be in our walk with the Lord.

Isn't it a relief to discover that getting your sentences to come out right isn't what prayer is about! Rather, prayer is simple, ongoing conversation with our heavenly Father that is honest and heartfelt. How exciting it is when we begin to discover that, through prayer, His goodness and power are changing lives—ours and those we've been praying for around the world.

Some books are meant to be read and laid aside. *31 Days of Prayer* is meant to be read and taken along through many months ahead in your journey with the Lord. I hope you'll do just that. This book will meet you right where you are and lead you closer to the Lord you love. May the Lord bless you on every page!

In His joy and peace,

Cliff Barrows

The Billy Graham Evangelistic Association

A Bit of History and Much Appreciation

Some time ago our friends at Multnomah Publishers asked my husband, Warren, and me to work with them on a new project—a companion to my book *31 Days of Praise*. Saying yes came easily, both to the subject and to the opportunity to write on prayer with Warren. Prayer—along with praise—has been a foundational emphasis in our lives and ministries for many years.

Besides the usual needs for prayer, I had been a widow with two young children for eight years. I can't imagine getting through those years without prayer—without talking with my Father, my Beloved. How often I brought to Him my deep inner needs and my perplexities. How often I prayed for my children and for the young women I was discipling and mentoring. Many of my most dramatic answers to prayer came during those years.

By the time I met Warren, he had long been known as a man of prayer. His time in the Word and in prayer was the highlight of his day. As his missionary work took him around Asia and the U.S., he would faithfully seek out a prayer partner. Or several. Sitting or kneeling, walking or driving, they would pray together about personal matters, about ministry opportunities, and about God's exciting worldwide purposes. I've sometimes thought that one of the many reasons he wanted to marry me was to have a permanent, almost-always-available prayer partner!

Together we wrote *Pray: How to Be Effective in Prayer* and *Praise: A Door to God's Presence.* And Warren was all-but-coauthor of *31 Days of Praise.* So the opportunity to work together on another prayer-mentoring book strongly appealed to us.

Our goal in *31 Days of Prayer* is to walk with you into a richer experience of praying—for yourself and others—and a growing closeness to God. To do this, we have written Scripture-based prayers for each day, similar to the praise portions in *31 Days of Praise.*

You'll notice the almost-daily presence of Andrew Murray, a favorite writer on the deeper life from a hundred years ago. (Our copy of his book *Abide in Christ* is dog-eared from use.) We've gleaned many ideas for prayer topics, along with a wealth of how-tos and other quotations, from Murray's works, especially his little gem on intercession, *Pray Without Ceasing.*

We trust this book will help your praying to grow deeper in faith, richer in content, and greater in breadth. It is our belief and experience that prayer changes our world—beginning, first of all, with the one who prays!

We're deeply grateful to the people of Multnomah Publishers who have helped make this book possible. We've been immensely helped by our editor, David Kopp, who did an excellent job of updating Murray's English as well as editing our material; it's been a joy to work with him. If we could, we would also express our thanks to Andrew Murray and the other men and women of God whom we have quoted.

Ruth Myers

AN INVITATION
TO PRAY

The telephone rings and it's your country's
leader. He wants to come by for a visit. While
you try not to gasp into the phone, he continues. He
hopes to find out if there's some way he can help
you. And he wants to talk personally with you about
a project on a scale almost beyond imagining—an
undertaking he'd like you to be a part of.

How would you feel after such a call?

"Well," you say, "I'd feel shocked, a bit
intimidated—and a bit doubtful about his motives."

Yes, but wouldn't you also feel honored?
Wouldn't your life suddenly seem more significant?
All your daily strivings a little less humdrum? As you
waited nervously for your president or prime
minister to visit, wouldn't you see yourself in a
completely different light?

The King of all kings, the Ruler of the entire
universe, has already made that call. He wants time

with you. He wants you to tell Him about your needs and interests. And He's asking for your partnership on an immensely important project.

If you've picked up this book, we're sure you're like so many Christians we've met. You sincerely long for that "closer, more fruitful walk with God." You also feel a deep concern for our hurting, disintegrating, fragmented world and the people in it—starting with your family, your friends, and your coworkers. And you want to be part of what God wants to do in people's lives and in our world.

What God has in mind begins with prayer. And His invitation to pray lies at the very heart of His loving best for each of us.

WHY GOD PLANNED PRAYER

Have you ever wondered why God chose to link His actions with our praying? Why did He decide that our prayers would cause Him to accomplish certain things or expand what He does? And that by not praying we would limit Him? Could He not have carried out His purposes far more efficiently without us? Yet He has established the prayers of His people as a powerful influence on how and when He meets our needs (material, emotional, spiritual) and the needs of others throughout the world.

The answer goes back to why God created us. He created us to be His loved ones, His family with whom He can share a relationship of mutual enjoyment. This shows the kind of God He is—a personal God who values loving relationships more than anything else in all the universe. Before He ever created angels and people, He was a "three-person" God—Father, Son, and Holy Spirit—living in perfect love and unbroken fellowship. He created us to be part of His inner circle of love, for both His delight and ours.

God longs to express His boundless love by meeting our needs to the point of overflowing. Even if we don't pray, He still holds together every molecule in our bodies; He is still the source of every good thing. But prayer keeps us aware of Him as our Source and opens our lives to receive His greater bounty. Prayer also links our lives with God's exciting purposes and power. More importantly, it brings us into a love relationship with God, rooted in our realizing how much we need Him and our choosing to depend on Him. The more we pray, the more we're able to let God meet our emotional and spiritual needs and love others through us. Prayer ushers us into an experience with God, with a growing sense of wonder, delight, and gratefulness.

The Rewards of "Giving" Prayers

Praying for others is a form of giving, and praying for God's best in our lives is part of giving ourselves to Him. As we form the habit of "giving" prayers, we start growing out of our natural tendency to major on "give me" prayers. We accept God's call to be partners with Him, with the high privilege of drawing people into His inner circle of love. We step into a larger arena of prayer, where we learn to pray more broadly, with God's purposes firmly in mind. We respond to the King's invitation when He said, "I'm up to something far more momentous than you might have supposed in your life, in the lives of your loved ones, and in the whole world—and I'm asking you to be part of it."

This lifts us out of the puny reasons for living that we humans invent apart from Him.

You may be wondering if there's something unacceptable about praying for everyday personal and family concerns—health, money, protection. Absolutely not. Jesus Himself taught us to pray, "Give us this day our daily bread." We follow His example when we acknowledge our need for God's down-to-earth favors and help.

God loves to hear you talk with Him about yourself and the people you love. He wants You to pray about your personal needs.

Yet this is not all there is to prayer. A child asking his dad for candy or a hamburger is not all there is to a growing relationship of love between him and his father. The Lord's Prayer has seven requests; six of them relate to God's purposes and to our spiritual needs, one to our practical needs. And the apostle Paul's prayers center largely on helping believers experience God and spiritual realities.

All kinds of prayers delight God—worship and thanksgiving, confessing our sins, quiet communion, praying for our own multilevel needs (often called petition), and praying for our loved ones and other people (intercession). All are part of mature praying—part of our wonderful privilege of conversing with the awesome, all-powerful Person who is our Father and our Friend.

The Privilege of Royal Praying

In the next thirty-one days, we also want to lead you into broader intercessory prayer—what we like to call "royal praying." It is praying along with the King of kings in His loving plans to bring relief and blessing and spiritual power to countless people. When we intercede we become prayer partners with Christ, who is always interceding before the Father (Hebrews 7:25). We join Him in His inner circle of prayer, where our prayers embrace His deepest longings as well as our own. And we get answers that make a tremendous difference now and forever.

Though we don't pray for others just to get blessed, intercessory prayer does bring extraordinary blessings our way. As always with God, we receive more than we give, and we become more than we are. We become part of the most significant undertaking of all time—the work of redemption that God has been doing for centuries. Breaking through the comfortable ways that fence us in, we gain a new sense of significance and fulfillment. And besides all this, we lay up tremendous rewards for eternity.

Jesus promised, "Give and it shall be given unto you." *Giving* prayer is one way of spending ourselves for others. It puts us in place to receive more of what God promises in many Scriptures, such as Isaiah 58:10–11: "If you spend yourselves in behalf of the hungry and satisfy the needs of the oppressed, then your light will rise in the darkness, and your night will become like the noonday. The LORD will guide you always; he will satisfy your needs in a sun-scorched land and will strengthen your frame. You will be like a well-watered garden, like a spring whose waters never fail" (NIV).

You Can Make a Difference

We believe *31 Days of Prayer* will help you. The message of this book has grown in our hearts over decades of praying, teaching on prayer, and writing about prayer. We believe this little book will motivate you to pray—and show you how. It will help you join others who have found that intercession makes impossible things possible, not only in our own households but also in faraway places.

For years in upper New York, a bedridden young woman prayed earnestly for a nomadic pygmy tribe in Africa. Ten years after she died, the tribe was reached by Gospel Recordings, Inc. with an incredible turning to Christ. For decades William Carey, considered the father of modern missions, sent detailed prayer requests from India to his invalid sister in England. She prayed over them with great diligence, and God used Carey in history-making ways.

In God's eyes, who gets the rewards for the amazing conversion of most of that pygmy tribe? And for Carey's remarkable work in India? We find a clue in 1 Samuel 30:24, where King David decreed, "The share of the man who stayed with the supplies is to be the same as that of him who went down to the battle. All will share alike" (NIV).

Early this century S. D. Gordon, the well-known devotional writer, wrote:

> The great people of the earth today are the people who pray. I do not mean those who talk about prayer; nor those who say they believe in prayer; nor yet those who can explain about prayer; but I mean those people who take time and pray. They have not time. It must be taken from something else. This something else is important. Very important, and pressing, but still less important and less pressing than prayer.

Two Lives Touched by Prayer

Because prayer is such an intimate experience, we want to give you a brief look at our personal stories.

It's been half a century since we began to understand and accept God's invitation to pray—

since we began to sense the wonder that God, the supreme Ruler of all, longs to hear our voices; that He cares about the things that concern us; and that He wants us, through prayer, to work with Him in His exciting purposes. God has been so gracious through the years in meeting our personal and ministry needs through prayer—sometimes through much prayer over many years.

Perhaps the most dramatic personal answer to prayer for both of us was the way God brought us together. Here's Warren's account, with a bit of background:

I came to Christ at the close of World War II. During the following year God gradually worked in my heart, making me willing to install Him as Lord of my life. The three issues I consciously surrendered to Him were my vocation, my location in the world, and my marriage. I was twenty-three at the time.

Over the next twenty years, in a variety of ways, God closed the door to several bright marriage prospects. Eventually I found myself attracted to Ruth, who had been a widow for over a year. I approached her about beginning a relationship. She was delighted with the idea—but not until seven years later. During that time, I prayed privately about her, I prayed with prayer partners, and I solicited prayer from friends.

Halfway through those seven years, I realized this relationship probably wasn't going to work out, so I gave up praying about it. But many others still felt this match was of the Lord and continued to carry the mantle of prayer. Finally, as Ruth says, the Lord warmed up her longtime respect for me with a deep love and a desire to marry me.

Sixteen years of waiting after I put marriage into the Lord's hands, then seven years after I approached Ruth—that made twenty-three years of waiting on God for a wife. Yet those years were not primarily years of waiting, for the Lord filled my life with many satisfactions and significant ways to serve Him—all in answer to prayer. But we're both immensely grateful that our prayer-hearing God answered in His perfect time.

Again and again down through the decades the Lord has put deep prayer burdens on our hearts over long periods of time—broad burdens for various countries and areas of the world, and specific burdens for individuals, with their great needs and potential. Many answers have come, many are still on their way, and many are spiritual changes that can't be measured.

On a broad scale, God answered countless prayers as He used us to pioneer the Navigator ministries in India, China, and other Asian countries. In one of those countries (unnamed here because of the continuing oppression of believers) the obstacles seemed like mountains. The only offer we could make to prospective team members was that after two years of full-time language study in the country, they might be able to get employment and visas to stay.

The Lord was true to His promise to guide us in unfamiliar paths (Isaiah 42:16). One by one, each of the families and single people found work and received a visa. Today more than fifty discipling professionals are at work in that country, sharing the good news and training nationals.

During Ruth's years as a widow, her most-treasured results of prayer came through quiet communing with God—with long pauses to let Him meet the needs of her heart. When she felt fearful or lonely, she'd go back to a favorite Scripture, like Isaiah 41:13. After talking with God about her feelings of loneliness, she would let Him speak the verse to her heart: "I, the LORD your God, will hold your right hand, saying to you, 'Fear not, I will help you'" (NKJV).

And Ruth would reply, "Lord, how I long to have someone hold my hand! And I've never had anyone better—and never will."

Or she'd say, "Lord, here I am again with my 'now-what-if' fears. But how can I go on fearing when You promise to hold my hand and help me?"

Then Ruth would extol Him for being so strong, so faithful, so delightful—and rest in the joy of what He is.

One of our greatest answers to prayer as a couple came through a problem our son, Brian, faced. As he was finishing high school in Singapore, he realized he was trapped in modern philosophies—the kind that led to nothingness and caused many a young person to commit suicide. More than four years crept by as we prayed and prayed. It was one of the most painful trials we've been through. Then in a marvelous way, half a world away, God answered prayer, restoring Brian to Himself. He's a pastor now, and his ministry with people is greatly enriched by those traumatic years.

These are some of the reasons why we wrote our books on prayer and praise. What an opportunity *31 Days of Prayer* has been to fulfill a basic ministry vision we have—to lead people along, step by step, into a closer, more fruitful walk with God.

God's Invitation to Success

When you thought of getting that phone call from your nation's top leader, perhaps you felt a bit fearful, a bit threatened. Maybe you feel the same way when you contemplate God's invitation to pray and intercede. The idea of adding yet another requirement to your hectic schedule sounds like just another setup for failure. "I'd love to pray more. But how?" you ask. "The last thing I need is more guilt!"

Perhaps you're in a season of life when more time for prayer seems like the impossible dream. Maybe you're a student with a heavy load, a mother with small children, a breadwinner working long hours, the caregiver for someone with a long-term illness or disability. Yet a richer prayer life can still be yours.

The good news is that we're not talking about spending hours in prayer. We're inviting you to invest ten to fifteen minutes a day to grow in prayer. And we'll show you how. Our aim is to encourage and help you, not to pressure you with guilt.

Sometimes God calls one of His children into an intensive, major ministry of prayer. Wonderful! Yet there's a blessed middle ground between intercession as a life work and no praying at all. In fact, we find there are many middle grounds in prayer that please the Lord. Like a loving earthly father, God always welcomes us into His presence, and He honors us when we show that we care and we try. Remember, prayer starts with a personal relationship, not with performance. Our fearful expectations probably come from our own confusion or from Satan, our day-and-night accuser (Revelation 12:10).

God's call to pray is an invitation to success. When we pray, we're succeeding in God's eyes. He then takes charge of the results of our praying, and He cannot fail. In His Word He has promised to hear and answer prayer. Our prayers may sometimes seem insignificant in our eyes, but they are not insignificant in God's eyes.

The time you can set aside for prayer may

seem small. But it will help you develop an attitude of prayer. Then you'll be able more and more to supplement your set-apart times of prayer with on-the-go prayers throughout the day. Many important answers to prayer come through such praying—and it can flourish in the busiest of schedules. Beginning to nurture some praying in your life, as it is right now, can become the launching pad for more later.

HELP ALONG THE WAY

God doesn't give a command, "Pray!" and then, like a drill sergeant, stand back to see if we'll obey, or come by only to inspect how well we're doing. He invites us—welcomes us—into the high privilege of talking and laboring with Him. He provides us with the enabling power of the Holy Spirit within us and gives us guidance for fruitful prayer in the Bible. He then encourages us through other Christians who may be a bit farther along the road than we are.

Consider this book part of the Lord's

encouragement to you. It will guide you in your new prayer adventure. It won't just tell you about prayer; it will actually lead you in prayer for thirty-one days—and, we trust, for months and even years. It will enhance your prayer life. It will also lead you into more vibrant spiritual health.

We have tried to make the book flexible and doable, not rigid and demanding. Whether you're a beginner in prayer or an experienced intercessor, we believe it will lead you, step by step, into praying about new things that are close to God's heart as well as those that are close to yours.

Most of all we pray that *31 Days of Prayer* will help fulfill God's highest reasons for prayer—that it will lift you, as one of His loved ones, to new heights, out of earthbound living and into the fresh air of His presence and a new awareness of the treasures He has stored up for all who love Him.

How to Use
the Days
of Prayer

God yearns for all of us to pray—but not for all of us to pray in exactly the same way. Many aspects of how we pray, and how much and how often, will depend on who we are and what our daily life is like.

The best way to learn to pray is by praying. Begin by setting apart time each day—ten or fifteen minutes—to pray through one of the day's entries. If you feel ill-prepared or inadequate, don't let that bother you. Instead, let it motivate you to depend on God for help to pray as He desires.

Use this book in a way that suits the personality and circumstances God has given you. And tailor your praying to fit the current stage of your spiritual growth.

In part 2 you'll find thirty-one written prayers, along with other helps and motivations for prayer. Because a meaningful prayer life grows naturally out of a healthy spiritual life, in part 3 we give more intensive help in several important areas of the Christian experience that directly impact prayer.

Each prayer help or suggestion in this book is simply an invitation—to greater significance and fulfillment in God's service. As you use the book, ask the Lord to help you grow into the kind of prayer life He wants for you.

Preparing for Prayer

After you open to each day's entry, begin by quieting your heart before the Lord. Meditate on the verse or two of Scripture given for the day's entry. Be still and know that He is God. Worship Him. These quiet moments can help you shift gears from other interests to God and His interests. They give the Holy Spirit a chance to distance your heart from the things of earth and fill it with peace and confidence in God.

Then use the "Daily Prayer of Expectancy" at the beginning of part 2. Consider this as your theme prayer, coming back to it often as you pray through the thirty-one days. This will help you express to the

Lord how you're depending on Him for your
continued growth in prayer. As you keep asking
Him to teach you to pray, He will keep on doing so.

PRAYING AND INTERCEDING

Now you're ready to pray through the written prayer
for the day. You may find that this helps you express
the things on your heart more clearly and freely,
with less mind wandering. Avoid rushing through
the prayer. Pause often to hold the requests before
the Lord. This will help you pray with your heart as
well as your mind.

You may wish to use the whole prayer just as it's
written, then bring to the Lord specific people and
needs you are especially concerned about. Or you
may find it easier to elaborate on the written
requests as you go, inserting additional concerns of
your own.

If you feel especially drawn to certain requests
in the prayer, pray longer for them, even if it means
neglecting others. And if you feel a prolonged
burden for a particular subject, consider praying

about it for several days before going on. You may want to come back to some days more often than once a month.

The prayers will help you pray for both yourself and others. They will bring to mind a broad range of needs and opportunities. They will encourage you to pray for people you know and people you don't, gradually drawing your heart out to all believers and to the whole world.

If at present some of the prayers seem too broad or too advanced, leave them for a future journey through the Days of Prayer.

Using a Prayer Journal

We encourage you to record prayer requests or your own written prayers in a prayer journal. This doesn't have to be anything fancy; a spiral-bound notebook works fine. Write down any specific prayer concerns the Lord lays on your heart, especially people you're close to. Add specific events and needs as they come to your attention. News programs and newspapers are a great source of fresh things to pray for.

Record answers as they come. As you review the answers, your faith will be strengthened and your heart will be filled with praise and joy. Find a method of journaling that is comfortable for you. Let your journaling reflect you and your walk with God.

Consider trying some of the following ideas:

- Jot down things that happen in your life, or in the lives of others, that give particular significance to the day's reading.
- Record praise items that the day's verses or quotations bring to mind.
- Write out some of the Scriptures referred to that day and your insights on them.
- Add other verses that come to mind, and tell why they're meaningful to you.
- Record your personal concerns and celebrations.
- Save meaningful quotations, song lyrics, or poetry.

You'll find it helpful to date each journal entry and answer to prayer. Then date new entries on each of your journeys through the thirty-one days.

That way you'll be creating both a personal journal and a personal history of praise and prayer.

Enriching Your Praying

The "As You Have Time" section can help you enrich and expand your praying as well. In this section you'll discover:

- a wealth of insights about how to pray;
- ideas to help you use God's Word in your prayers;
- inspiring quotations, poems, and lyrics;
- mentoring in such prayer-enhancing areas as knowing God better and loving others more.

Consider focusing on different entries in "As You Have Time" each time you pray through the thirty-one days.

Prayer isn't just something else on your to-do list, but an expression of an ever-deepening walk with God. Throughout part 2 you'll be referred to part 3, "Ways to Grow in Prayer," for help in key areas of a maturing, flourishing relationship with God.

You will find our earlier book, *31 Days of Praise,* an excellent companion for this book. You might consider using the prayer book during a regular set-apart time—then dipping into the praise book first thing in the morning, during a break in your day, or before bed. Or use the books on alternate months.

We pray that He will guide you in just how you can best use these days of prayer. Day by day, month by month, may prayer increase your delight in God and help you influence others to love and honor Him.

DAILY PRAYER OF EXPECTANCY

Father in heaven, great and powerful and full of love, I lift my heart in praise for the privilege of coming to You in prayer. Give me special grace as I join Your exalted Son in His ministry of prayer.

Search my heart, Lord, and show me if any sin is hindering Your work in my life. May I respond without delay whenever You make me conscious of sin. How grateful I am for Your total forgiveness the moment I confess my sin, turning back to You as my Lord!

And Father, teach me to pray. How much I yearn to know Your will and Your way. I thank You that Your Son lives within me. What a joy to know that He is my teacher—that through Him I can learn to pray. I can learn to release Your boundless power for both my needs and the needs of many others, near and far. Teach me to pray.

Day by day may Your Spirit work in me, motivating me to abide in Christ and pray in faith, moving Your mighty hand to fulfill Your purposes. Keep reminding me that You are able to do infinitely more than I would ever dare to ask or imagine, by Your mighty power at work within me.

To You be the glory both now and forever. Amen.

PRAY FOR GOD'S BLESSING
ON YOUR WORK AND
DAILY ACTIVITIES.

Lord, my highest good is to have You near.
And how wonderful that You want me to
come near to You—that You delight to see my face
and hear my voice. You want me to walk close to
You all day long, resting my heart in the joy of who
You are. Enable me to do this more and more.

How good of You, gracious Master, to call all
Your children to serve as Your ambassadors in all
that we do. How encouraging to know that every
task I undertake as Your servant is Your work, even
my small tasks! And that through prayer I can put
You into all my daily activities—my employment,
my marriage, my parenting, my spiritual walk and
service, my free time and hobbies.

I commit all I do into Your hands and ask You
to work in and through me. Give me grace to do

*D*raw near to God and He will draw
near to you.

JAMES 4:8

each of my tasks for You, putting my whole heart
into it. Keep me depending on You for strength and
wisdom all day long. (Pray specifically about various
things you'll be doing.)

Lord, You alone can give true significance to
my work and activities. So I call on You to prosper
all that I do. Let Your favor be upon me, and give
permanence to what I do.

May I spread the fragrance of Christ to everyone
my life touches day by day. Make me a gracious
witness to those who don't know You, and a blessing
to those who do.

Scripture References (by paragraph)

1. Psalm 73:28
2. 2 Corinthians 5:20
3. Proverbs 16:3; Philippians 2:13; Colossians 3:23–24;
   Philippians 4:13; James 1:5
4. Psalm 127:1; 1:2–3; 90:17 (marginal note)
5. 2 Corinthians 2:14–16

As You Have Time

Enjoying God's nearness. "The nearness of God gives us rest and power in prayer. This nearness is given to the person who makes God's intimate presence a priority. Seek nearness to God and He will give it, 'He will draw near to you.' God's nearness makes it easy to pray in faith. So persevere. Learn to place yourself in His presence, quietly anticipate His drawing near, then begin to pray." Andrew Murray

Prayer and work. "I am convinced that God does not wish us to neglect rightful work to pray. But it is equally certain that we might work better and do more work if we gave less time to work and more to prayer." The Unknown Christian

Open for what He assigns. Here's a motto for all of us in all we do: "God's will, nothing more, nothing less, nothing else." Pray that you will be open to whatever the Lord wants you to do day by day. Tell Him you simply want to be used by Him, whether in great tasks or lowly ones, whether the results will seem large or small.

PRAY FOR A LIFE OF ABIDING
IN CHRIST.

Dear Father, what a privilege it is to abide in
Christ—to dwell in Him, sharing His life as a
branch shares the life of a vine! Thank You that He is
my life.

Work in my heart to keep me abiding in Christ
and filled with His Spirit day by day and moment by
moment, by simple faith. Show me any hindrances
to this in my life, and enable me to fling them aside.
May His Word live in me richly; may I keep His
commandments and abide in His love. May I so
fully identify with Him as the Vine that people
around will see in me His nature and His life. Lord,
may this be especially true in my relationships and
work, my marriage and family life.

I pray these same things for the believers in my
church and for other believers I know, especially
_____ and _____. May the truths about
abiding in Christ dawn on each of us in a fresh way.

"If you abide in Me, and My words abide in you, ask whatever you wish, and it shall be done for you."

JOHN 15:7

In our living and our praying, may we fully depend on Him, just as He fully depended on You.

Scripture References (by paragraph)

1. John 15:4–5; Colossians 3:4
2. Ephesians 5:18; Galatians 2:20; Hebrews 12:1;
   John 15:7; Colossians 3:16; John 15:10
3. John 14:10

AS YOU HAVE TIME

ABIDING IN CHRIST. "Our acceptance with God and our access to Him is through Christ. As we consciously abide in Him, we are free from the power of our old nature. In this divine freedom from self-will, we are free to ask God for what we want, being influenced now by our new nature. And God will do it. Let us treasure this place of freedom through abiding in Christ—and believe that our requests right now are heard and will be answered." Andrew Murray

We find a night-and-day difference in our lives when we choose against struggling to be strong and peaceful and loving—and instead, count on the strength and peace and love of Christ's life within us. And how good it is to know that abiding in Christ is not an unusual, added extra in the Christian life intended for a few "special" Christians. It's part of God's plan for each of His children.

For more about this see the section "Abide in Christ" on page 184.

PRAY FOR PERSONAL NEEDS AND
DESIRES, WITH THANKSGIVING.

Father, thank You that I can come to You
with simple confidence, as a little child comes
to his father or mother asking for what he needs.
What a gracious, generous Father You are!

I'm so grateful to You for giving me life and
breath and everything else. Every good and perfect
gift comes from You, the Creator of all lights, more
constant and unchanging than the sun and moon
and stars. You are a sun and a shield, bringing light
and warmth into my life and protecting me from
harm. You've promised that I won't lack anything
good—that I'll be safe and secure without fear of
harm—if I seek You with a reverent heart, if I
choose to trust You and go Your way instead of my
own. More and more, make me this kind of person.

Help me praise You often for Your great
goodness and tender love and trust You more for all

$\mathcal{Y}$ou can throw the whole weight of your anxieties on him, for you are his personal concern.

1 PETER 5:7, PHILLIPS

that I need. I come to You now with my needs and desires. Draw me close to You as I bring them to You day by day.

I pray about my need for encouragement...for release from inner stress...for greater love and wisdom in relating to others, especially my family...for knowing how to handle my insecurities, my anxieties, my anger...for open doors in the future. I also pray for the needs of my parents...my brothers and sisters...my marriage partner and my marriage itself...my coworkers...my neighbors. Lord, work in special ways.

Thank You, Lord, that You are "so vastly wonderful, so utterly and completely delightful, that You can meet and overflow the deepest needs of my total nature, mysterious and deep as that nature is" (A. W. Tozer).

Scripture References (by paragraph)

1. Luke 11:11–13
2. Acts 17:25; 1 Timothy 6:17; James 1:17; Malachi 3:6;
   Psalm 84:11; 34:9–10; Proverbs 1:33
3. Psalm 118:1; James 4:8

As You Have Time

THE DETAILS MATTER TO GOD. "Tell God every detail
of your needs in thankful prayer" (Philippians 4:6,
Phillips). God cares deeply about you and wants you
to talk to Him about all that concerns you. Record
in a notebook your practical and emotional needs—
and those of your family and friends. As missionary
Rosalind Goforth wrote, "There is nothing too
great for His power, and nothing too small for His
love."

Remember to write down the answers as they
come. Your faith will grow, and you'll be reminded

to thank your Father for what He does.

A YIELDING SPIRIT. Be careful not to pray with a demanding or complaining attitude. During their desert wanderings, the Israelites grumbled about the food God was providing each day. They craved meat—and insisted on getting it. Psalm 106:15, KJV, tells the result: "He gave them their request; but sent leanness into their soul." They lost far more than they gained.

Paul prayed repeatedly that his "thorn in the flesh" would be removed, believing that to be God's will. Then God told him it was better for him to have the thorn, that His strength would be completed through Paul's weakness (2 Corinthians 12:7–10).

Paul prayed for something that was not God's will. Why didn't God chasten him? Because, above all else, Paul wanted to please God. He was mistaken about God's will, but his heart was right.

PRAY FOR WISDOM AND
GUIDANCE.

Dear Lord, how generous and powerful You
are! Able to listen to and help everyone in the
world at the same time. What a wonderful Master
to belong to! And thank You for revealing Your
promises, commands, and principles, so that Your
Spirit can guide me in my praying and in my living.

I come to You now, asking You for greater
wisdom and understanding in spiritual things. May
I know what You want for me in the important
decisions I'm facing. Give me on-the-spot wisdom
in conversations and in immediate decisions. In
such decisions enable me to quickly commit them to
You and trust You to help me say and do the right
thing. Keep reminding me to do this, both at home
and elsewhere so that I won't depend on my own
understanding.

Guide me in the long-range decisions I'm
facing. Help me seek the Holy Spirit's

$\mathcal{W}$e can be confident that he will listen to us whenever we ask him for anything in line with his will. And...we can be sure that he will give us what we ask for.

1 JOHN 5:14–15, NLT

enlightenment from Your Word. Help me as I weigh the possibilities, then conclude the right steps to take and the right time to take them. How much I need Your wisdom and guidance!

I pray now about some special decisions I have to make regarding _____ and _____ . And guide other believers, near and far, in the decisions they are facing—especially _____ , and _____ . As our Shepherd, lead us in good paths, in paths that please You.

Again I praise You for Your wonderful wisdom and power and Your deep desire for my highest good—each day and throughout my whole life.

Scripture References (by paragraph)

1. Psalm 145:6–7; 16–19
2. Colossians 1:9–11, NCV; Psalm 37:5; Proverbs 3:5–6
3. 2 Chronicles 20:12
4. Psalm 33:3; 143:8–10
5. Isaiah 55:8–9; Ephesians 3:20; Romans 8:28–29

As You Have Time

AGREEING WITH WHAT GOD WANTS. How can we know what God wants us to ask for? Primarily through His Word, the Bible. When we know something is according to His Word, we can pray with confident faith. George Mueller wrote, "Faith is not a matter of impressions or probabilities or appearances. Faith is the assurance that what God has said in His Word is true, and that God will act accordingly. This confidence is faith."

IF-IT-IS-YOUR-WILL PRAYERS. At times prayers which request extras we're not fully assured are God's will are part of our friendship with the Lord. We ask; we hold our desires in open hands, refusing to grasp or insist; and God answers. Sometimes He fulfills our desires, sometimes He asks us to wait, sometimes He refuses our requests so that He can give us something better. Aren't we at times like a small child who wants to play with a shiny, sharp knife? What does Mom do? She gives the child something safer, something better.

DISCERNING GOD'S WILL THROUGH HIS WORD. You can find God's will for your praying not only through His promises and commands in Scripture, but also through the truths, principles, and examples He has revealed there. The more familiar you become with His wonderful Word, the more you will know His ways of thinking. Then you can pray with increased confidence that you're asking for what He wants. And in areas not clearly covered in the Bible, you can more readily discern whether you're being prompted by the Spirit or by your own feelings and impressions.

PRAY ABOUT YOUR TRIALS
AND TESTINGS.

Father, I worship before You as the sovereign
God, the Blessed Controller of all things. You
always want what is best, You always know what is
best, and You're always able to do what is best for
Your obedient, trusting children. Nothing is too
hard for You.

I rejoice that You promise to cause all things—
even things that are contrary to Your ideal will—to
fit into a pattern for good for those who love You.
And that this "good" includes becoming more like
Jesus! And that somehow my prayers can make a
difference in how things turn out and how much I
benefit from all that comes my way. Thank You for
Your promise, "Call upon Me in the day of trouble; I
will deliver you and you will honor Me."

Give me grace, Lord, to trust You in each of my
trials, large or small—to accept each one and

But I call to God, and the LORD saves me.
Evening, morning and noon I cry out in
distress, and he hears my voice.

PSALM 55:16-17, NIV

cooperate with You so that I'll grow through it.

Guide me as I bring each problem area to
You—my pressures, my finances, my uncertainties,
my disappointments and failures (including my
failures in relating to people). I trust You to work in
my situations and give me practical wisdom in how
to handle them. And even more, work in me. I lack
power and I don't know what to do, but my eyes are
on You.

Do these same things for _____ and
_____ in their trials.

Scripture References (by paragraph)

1. 1 Timothy 6:15, Phillips; Jeremiah 29:11; 32:17;
   Luke 1:37
2. Romans 8:28–29; Psalm 34:6; 50:15
3. 2 Corinthians 12:9; James 1:2–5; Psalm 37:5–6
4. 2 Chronicles 20:12

As You Have Time

DON'T BE SURPRISED OR BEWILDERED. Trials are not abnormal experiences (1 Peter 4:12). Whether God actually sends them or simply allows them to happen, they are part of His plan for removing ugly qualities from us and developing beautiful, Christlike lives. That's why Job could say in the midst of devastating trials, "When He has tried me, I shall come forth as gold" (Job 23:10). Centuries later James wrote, "You have heard of the endurance of Job and have seen the outcome of the Lord's dealings, that the Lord is full of compassion and is merciful" (James 5:11).

PRAYING IN JESUS' NAME AND MERITS. "God exalted Him to the highest place and gave Him the name that is above every name" (Philippians 2:9, NIV). Only through Jesus' name can we approach

God. He died on the cross to pay the full penalty for all our sins and make us acceptable to God. And we received these benefits by faith alone; what Jesus did was enough. Now we do not pray in our own name or worth. ("Lord, You should answer my prayers because I've been reading my Bible and living a good life.")

Instead, we approach Him solely in His name, trusting in who He is and what He has done: "Thank You, Lord Jesus, that as a 'Christ-follower' I am called by Your noble and wonderful name. By Your undeserved favor, I have been made a member of Your royal family. Now I can approach You boldly, in Your merits alone. I expect You to answer my prayers because I come in Your name, concerned about what You want. What a privileged beggar I am!"

PRAY FOR THE WORD OF GOD
TO BUILD YOU UP.

Dear Lord, work in me so that I will always be alert and thankful when I pray, whether alone or with others. So much depends on prayer! Don't let me be careless, or distracted, or on-and-off in my praying.

May the same be true as I immerse myself in Your Word. I praise You for inspiring this marvelous book to build us up and set us free. How glad I am for the way it keeps me on track in my praying and my living!

May I look intently into Your Word day by day with a longing to know You better and do Your will at all times. May the Spirit unfold its truths to me; may He motivate me to meditate on it and apply it to my life. Make me diligent to hear and read it often, to make notes on it, to memorize it. Empower me to trust You and obey all Your commands. May Your Word be the joy and rejoicing of my heart.

"*If* you believe, you will receive whatever you ask for in prayer."

MATTHEW 21:22

Strengthen and renew me (and _____ and _____) through Your Word, keeping us from sin—so that time after time we may know the refreshment that comes from Your presence. Give us gracious boldness and power to share it with others, both believers and unbelievers.

I pray for Your rich blessing on Bible distribution, as well as on Bible preaching, teaching, and reading in our area—and beyond. Give special grace to those in countries where Bibles are scarce. May every child of Yours somehow get at least a New Testament and be nourished by its truths.

Scripture References (by paragraph)

1. Colossians 2:4
2. 2 Timothy 3:16–17; Acts 20:32; John 8:31–32
3. James 1:25; Philippians 3:10; Joshua 1:8; Isaiah 50:4; Deuteronomy 17:19; Jeremiah 15:16
4. Psalm 119:25, 28, 11; Acts 3:19, Phillips; Colossians 3:16; 4:5–6

As You Have Time

Honoring God with faith. God wants you to trust His love, power, and faithfulness and believe He will answer your prayers. When doubts creep in, bring them honestly to God. Be like the man who told Jesus, "Lord, I believe; help my unbelief" (Mark 9:24, NKJV). Often the Lord increases our faith by answering our prayers, even though our faith is weak. But He wants us to pray with a growing faith, not just with wishes and hopes. Beware of doubting that you *want* God's way and help. "That [double-minded] man should not think he will receive anything from the Lord" (James 1:7).

"To believe that the Lord will hear my prayer honors His truthfulness, His power, His love and generosity, His wisdom. If you wish to dishonor every attribute of God, pray with unbelief. But if you want to put a crown on the head of Him who has saved you, believe that if you ask He will give" (C. H. Spurgeon).

"WE" AND "US" PRAYERS. Notice how Daniel identified with God's people as he prayed for them, using "we" prayers rather than "they" prayers (Daniel 9:4–19). And Jesus taught His disciples to pray "us" prayers—"Lead us not into temptation" (Matthew 6:13, NIV). Moses prayed a fresh and simple "us" prayer in Psalm 90:14, "Satisfy us in the morning with Your unfailing love" (NIV).

As you pray, your "us" can start with you and your spouse or closest friend; then you and your family; then in a widening circle finally encompass all believers.

PRAY ABOUT LORDSHIP AND
PROTECTION FROM EVIL.

Loving Father, faithful and full of power, I'm
so grateful I can come to You with
confidence, for You keep Your promises and answer
prayer. Not one single word of Your good promises
has ever failed.

Lord, I submit myself to You, presenting my life
and my desires as a living sacrifice. I acknowledge
You as Lord of my desires, my plans, my successes
and failures, my place in the world, my friendships,
my popularity. You are Lord of my present and future
relationships, health, money, possessions, and human
approval. How good it is to yield to You, knowing
that You withhold no good thing from Your
obedient children who trust You and call on You.

I choose to give up all right to myself, take up my
cross day by day, and follow You. Give me power to
resist the devil. Give me grace not to let the world

*S*o brothers and sisters, since God has shown us great mercy, I beg you to offer your lives as a living sacrifice to him.

squeeze me into its mold—its desire to indulge...its desire to possess...its desire to impress. Instead, may Your Spirit remold my mind from within. I really need this, Father, so that I can know You better, delight in You more constantly, and experience Your good and perfect will for me.

Show Your mighty power, Lord, by keeping me following You closely. Do the same for my Christian friends and family members, especially the young ones. Deliver us from sin and from Satan. Do this especially for those who right now are toying with temptation or giving in to sin.

May we steer clear of sin, but don't let us isolate ourselves from the people of the world. Motivate us to reach out in love to them—to our relatives, friends, neighbors, and associates—as Your lights shining in a dark place.

Scripture References (by paragraph)

1. 1 Kings 8:56
2. James 4:7; Romans 12:1–2; Psalm 84:11–12;
   James 4:7; Luke 9:23; 1 John 2:15–16
3. Matthew 6:13
4. Philippians 2:15

AS YOU HAVE TIME

ANYWHERE ON LIFE'S CHECKERBOARD. Are you ready to put yourself fully at the disposal of your gracious, merciful Lord who sacrificed His life for you? Are you willing to give up the things you want and surrender yourself daily to follow Jesus? We like this quote from an unknown author:

> Simply to drop all our dreams and
> ambitions and preferences, and to have no
> mind about it at all, but be willing for God
> to shift us anywhere on life's checker-
> board, or bury us anywhere in life's garden,
> counting not our lives dear and loving

them not unto death, gladly yielding
ourselves for God to please Himself with,
anywhere and anyway He chooses—that is
rarely done.

If you are hesitant to drop your dreams and
preferences into the loving hands of God, ask Him to
work in you and make you willing (Philippians 2:13).
Ask Him to nurture in His people everywhere the
glad response of the hymn writer, "Ready to go, ready
to stay, ready my place to fill...ready to do Your will."

Pray also that this surrender will not be short-
lived but lifelong, renewed quickly if reservations
slip in. In *Shadow of the Almighty,* Jim Elliott said, "One
does not surrender a life in an instant; that which is
lifelong can only be surrendered in a lifetime."

Commitment to Christ, like marriage, is one
big yes and a lot of little uh-huhs along the way.

PRAY FOR LOVE AND AGAINST
HINDRANCES.

Lord of love, You are the one Source of
perfect, unfailing love. Love that is sacrificial,
imparatial, and permanent! Work in me a growing
love and affection for all people, and especially for all
believers—a love like Yours: merciful,
compassionate, ready to forgive, patient, considerate,
deeply concerned about others' well-being.

Show me if there's anything in my heart that
would keep me from praying with Your love. Do You
see grievances there? Anger? An unforgiving spirit?
Resentment toward anyone in my past, or in my
present? Envy or jealousy? Critical attitudes?
Selfishness or pride? Anything else that hinders love?
Show me. And give me grace to repent and ask You to
forgive me. Help me take the initiative in restoring any
broken or damaged relationships with others in my
family, at work, or at my church.

May the Spirit flood my heart with Your love,

*A*lways keep on praying for all the saints.

EPHESIANS 6:18, NIV

washing away any unloving attitudes. Then may Your pure, warm love motivate me as I pray and flow through me toward every person my life touches day by day. I plead with You for this! And I believe You will do it.

And Lord, do these same things for all who partner with You in prayer, wherever they may be.

Scripture References (by paragraph)

1. 1 John 4:7–19; 1 Thessalonians 3:12; Philippians 1:9; Psalm 86:5; 145:8–9; Matthew 5:44–45
2. Psalm 139:23–24; Hebrews 12:15; Philippians 2:3–4; Ephesians 4:26, 31–32; Matthew 5:23–24
3. Romans 5:5, Phillips

AS YOU HAVE TIME

LOVE FOR OTHERS. "If we are to pray for others, we must love. Every part of a body is interested in the welfare of the whole, and exists to complete and help the other parts. Believers are one body, and we ought to pray for the welfare of all Christ's followers." Andrew Murray

PRAY SPECIFICALLY, WITHOUT JUDGING. We can be more specific in prayer for other believers than just, "Lord, bless them..." Here are some requests for other believers. Pray that:

* their supreme desire will be to know and glorify Christ.
* their roots will go deep into Christ and His Word.
* they will realize the rich blessings lavished on them in Christ.
* they will truly abide in Christ, obeying Him by the Spirit's power.
* they will be a fragrance of Christ to unbelievers, able and ready to share His Word in appropriate and timely ways.

For more help, see "Pray with a Nonjudgmental Attitude," page 199.

PRAY FOR STRENGTH AND
WELL-BEING.

Dear Father, I worship You as the One who
made me, who intricately fashioned me as a
unique person, weaving me with great skill in my
mother's womb. By Your gracious, unlimited power
You hold together all things—including each cell of
my body.

Today, by Your Spirit within me, I'm counting
on You to bring to my whole being new strength
and vitality—physical and emotional strength,
spiritual and moral strength. Strength to do Your
will.

And Lord, give me peace—*shalom*—wholeness
and harmony and well-being. Bring emotional
strength and joy day by day. In times of need give
me grace to pour out my heart to You and cast on
You all my anxieties and stresses and tensions. And
then to fix my thoughts on You and rest in You. I
pray these things for myself, Lord, and for others in

The God of Israel gives his people strength
and power.

PSALM 68:35, NCV

need—including _____. Where there is
weakness, may there be strength—Your strength.
Where there is sickness, may there be healing. You
are the One who heals us. "Man treats, God heals."
May Your healing touch be on our bodies until the
time comes when You choose to bring us total
healing by calling us Home.

Day by day, may I rest my faith in Your tender
love and Your infinite wisdom—Your deep,
unsearchable wisdom. With quiet faith I trust You
for health and healing, confident and expectant. But
keep me from demanding, from clenching my
fingers around what I think is best for me and
others. May I honor You by affirming, "Our God
whom we serve is able to deliver us, and He will
deliver us. But even if He does not, we will still trust
Him."

Most of all I pray for spiritual health. Keep me

simply trusting You, yielding to You, and honoring
You in all I am and all I do and think and say.

Scripture References (by paragraph)

1. Psalm 139:13–16; Colossians 1:16–17
2. Romans 8:11, Phillips; Psalm 59:17; Isaiah 33:2
3. Isaiah 26:3; Psalm 62:8; 1 Peter 5:7;
   2 Corinthians 12:9–10; Psalm 103:3; Malachi 4:2;
   3 John 2; Psalm 116:15
4. Romans 11:33–34; Daniel 3:17–18

AS YOU HAVE TIME

THE STRENGTH OF HUMILITY. "You may be feeling
unworthy and unable to pray as you know you
should. Accept this heartily, and be content to come
to God anyway and be blessed in your unworthiness,
simply trusting God's grace. This is true humility.
Humility is the strength behind a great faith, and
leads to answered prayers. Don't let your 'littleness'
hinder your prayers for a moment." Andrew Murray

For more on humility and effective prayer, see

"Walk Humbly with Your God," page 189.

Strength and health through God and His Word. George Mueller lived ninety-two years, with amazing strength and health to the end. Arthur T. Pierson reports that Mueller attributed his health and long life to three causes:

1. His striving to always keep his conscience clear before God and man (Acts 24:16)
2. His love for the Scriptures, and the way they constantly restored his whole being, even his body (Proverbs 3:2, 8; 4:22)
3. His happiness in God and His work, which relieved him of all anxiety and needless wear and tear in his labors (Psalm 55:22)

PRAY THAT MANY WILL TURN
TO CHRIST.

Lord, I bow humbly before You. You are high
and exalted, and I am so small and so human,
so limited by time and space. You are holy and I fall
so far short of Your glorious ideals. What amazing
grace that You grant me access to You at all times,
day and night!

Show me afresh Your deep love for the world—
Your yearning that people trust Christ and live with
You forever in Your eternal family. To think that my
prayers can help fulfill Your longings!

I desire to persevere in prayer day by day for
my unsaved family members and friends, including
especially _____, _____, and
_____. Give me grace to pray for them
often, and to relate to them with greater love and
helpfulness, and to tell them of Christ in winsome
and timely ways. Make them intensely aware of their
need for forgiveness. Convince them of Your love

"*To* open their eyes and turn them from darkness to light, and from the power of Satan to God, so that they may receive forgiveness of sins...by faith in me."

ACTS 26:18, NIV

and draw them to Christ. Do the same for my friends and more distant relatives who don't know You, including _____ and _____.

It seems, Lord, that there are so many barriers that keep people from You. Deliver those who think there are no absolutes, who believe that every viewpoint or lifestyle is okay as long as it seems right to them. Turn people from modern philosophies and Eastern religious practices—and from pursuing ideals of some sort (even "Christian" goodness or service), depending on their own efforts rather than on Christ. Defeat Satan as he blinds them to their need of the Cross. Open the eyes of thousands daily to the glorious light of the Good News of Christ. May many trust You for forgiveness in our community, our region, and beyond.

Show me how and where to focus my prayers.

And motivate many around the world to pray
faithfully that people will come to Christ.

Scripture References (by paragraph)

1. Isaiah 57:15; Romans 3:23; Ephesians 3:12
2. Romans 5:8; 2 Peter 3:9
3. Luke 11:5–10; 1 Timothy 2:1, 3–4; Matthew 5:16;
    Colossians 4:5–6; John 6:44
4. Isaiah 5:20–21; Colossians 2:8; Romans 10:2–3;
    2 Corinthians 4:3–4; Acts 26:18

As You Have Time

YOUR PRAYERS ARE IMPORTANT. "Don't think that you
have no influence, or that your prayers are not
important. Your prayers and faith will make a
difference." Andrew Murray

NEVER GIVE UP. George Mueller is renowned for
his many, often-dramatic answers to prayer, and for
the way he carefully sought God's mind in what he
prayed for. Yet he prayed for years that certain

people would be converted, and the answers came very slowly, one by one. He wrote:

> The great point is never to give up until the answer comes. I have been praying for fifty-two years, every day, for two men, sons of a friend of my youth. They are not converted yet, but they will be!... The great fault of the children of God is, they do not continue in prayer; they do not go on praying; they do not persevere. If they desire anything for God's glory, they should pray until they get it.

PRAY FOR THE HOLY SPIRIT'S
FULL MINISTRY IN YOU
AND OTHERS.

Thank You, my wonderful Father, the Source of
every good and perfect gift, that You have sent
Your Spirit to live in me—as a fountain of living water
within me, springing up to refresh my heart and
renew my mind. How sufficient His power is for my
needs and for the needs of all Your children! Thank
You for Your promise of His ministry in our lives day
by day, as we continue to ask and seek and knock.

I yield, Lord, to Your Spirit. I pray that He will
fill me today and minister to me and through me.
May He enlighten and nourish me through Your
Word, strengthen my inner person, and fill my heart
to overflowing with Your love. May He produce in
me the very temperament of Jesus—His ways of
thinking and behaving and reacting. Father, may this
be especially true in my relationships—family and
otherwise—in which I'm most prone to act and
react in unloving ways.

I pray that out of his glorious riches he may strengthen you with power through his Spirit in your inner being.

I pray that the Spirit will empower me to witness with boldness. Wherever I may be, may He flow out from my inmost being as refreshing rivers of living water, meeting the needs of others. Help me depend on Him as I pray, counting on His presence within me, interceding for me and along with me. How much better He is than even my best and closest prayer partner!

I plead with You, Lord, for these same ministries of the Spirit in my prayer partners and in others who pray for Your work around the globe.

How much we need a revival of prayer, so that Christ's great commission will be fulfilled in all the world. Lord, bring one!

Scripture References (by paragraph)

1. James 1:17; John 4:14; Luke 11:9–13; Ephesians 5:18; John 14:26; 16:13–14
2. Ephesians 3:16; Romans 5:5; 2 Corinthians 3:18; Galatians 5:22–23
3. Acts 1:8; John 7:37–39; Romans 8:26–27

As You Have Time

THE HELP OF THE HOLY SPIRIT. "The Holy Spirit helps us.... For we don't even know what we should pray for, nor how we should pray" (Romans 8:26, NLT). When you feel ignorant and weak in your praying, you can trust in the indwelling and intercession of the Holy Spirit within you. Make a habit of yielding yourself to His life in you and His leading. He will help you in your prayer weaknesses. Andrew Murray advised, "Pray with the simplicity of a little child. Pray with the holy awe and reverence of one in whom God's Spirit always dwells and prays."

Breathe on me, Breath of God,
Fill me with life anew,
That I may love what Thou dost love,
and do what Thou wouldst do.
Breathe on me, Breath of God,

Till I am wholly Thine,
Until this earthly part of me
Glows with the fire divine.

EDWIN HATCH

STRENGTH FOR PRAYER. Intercession is not easy. It requires supernatural strength. So our praying must not be by our own might or power, but by the Lord's Spirit (Zechariah 4:6). Choose to depend completely on God, drawing on His strength to help you pray. Offer praise that the Spirit of the all-powerful God who raised Christ from the dead lives in you. What vast resources of strength you have for all God wants you to do!

Savor other verses that speak to you about being strengthened by the Lord, such as Ephesians 6:10; Philippians 4:13; Isaiah 33:2; 40:29–31; 41:10.

PRAY FOR GOD'S WORKING IN
YOUR CHURCH.

Father, thank You for the privilege of
fellowship with brothers and sisters in Your
family. Some are such caring and encouraging
Christians, helping fellow believers grow, reaching
out to the lost, and serving in countless ways.
Others need a greater interest in You and Your
loving purposes. Work in me, making me faithful to
pray regularly for them, in view of how dear they
are to You.

Lord, may I, and each of us in our church, grow
in Your grace and in the knowledge of Your Son. In
each service may we be worshipful and attentive,
eager to learn and change our ways. And may we
learn to use our spiritual gifts and serve as You lead.

Protect us from being deceived and led astray.
Help us with our doubts, our stresses, our trials, and
our relationships, especially in our families. Make
our love for You and for one another increase and

Let us...spur one another on toward love and good deeds.... Let us encourage one another.

HEBREWS 10:24–25, NIV

overflow. May those who have disputes or grievances resolve them quickly, before the end of the day. I pray these same things for our church's leaders and workers. In new ways make us a glory to Your name.

May we so live together in harmony, both in our families and our church, that our unity will be like a sweet perfume to You and to others, both believers and unbelievers.

Scripture References (by paragraph)

1. 1 John 1:3; Hebrews 10:24–26; Matthew 4:10; 20:26–28; John 17:23
2. 2 Peter 3:18; James 1:22–25; Romans 12:4–8
3. Ephesians 4:14; 1 Thessalonians 3:12; Matthew 5:23–24; Ephesians 4:26
4. Psalm 133

As You Have Time

Your church family. Andrew Murray wrote: "Each of us is connected with some church or circle of believers who represent most directly Christ's body to us. They have a special claim on our prayers, so pray regularly about their needs. Find others of like mind to join with you in private, specific petitions."

The anonymous writer of the following lines reminds us of God's perspective:

> Oh that when Christians
> meet and part,
> These words were carved
> on every heart—
> They're dear to God!
> However willful and unwise,
> We'll look on them with loving eyes—
> They're dear to God!
> O wonder!—to the Eternal One,

Dear as His own beloved Son;
Dearer to Jesus than His blood;
Dear as the Spirit's fixed abode—
They're dear to God!

PRAYING ALOUD WITH OTHERS. Praying aloud with others is a tangible way for you to carry your load—and bring encouragement. If it's hard for you to pray aloud in a group, begin by doing it when you pray alone. Then start praying aloud with a friend. Don't compare your praying with others. William Gurnall wrote: "Sometimes you hear another pray with freedom and fluency, while you can hardly get out a few broken words. Hence you are ready to accuse yourself and admire him, as if the gilding of the key makes it open the door better."

PRAY FOR SUNDAY SCHOOLS AND
BIBLE STUDY GROUPS.

Gracious Father—High King of heaven, yet
my Father!—You are seated in the throne
room of the universe on a throne of grace, a throne
of favor for the undeserving. What a privilege it is to
come to Your throne unafraid, with utter freedom
and confidence, assured of Your glad welcome—"to
run right into Your throne room and find Your arms
open wide!" (Kay Arthur). To know that I'll find
mercy for my failures and grace for my every need!
What good news that I don't need to be almost
perfect to come boldly into Your presence! Your
mercy lets me come with my mistakes, my sins, my
needs—as long as I come honestly. Thank You that
You are always ready to forgive, always eager to hear
my voice and answer my prayers.

Thank You, Lord, for the dedicated Sunday
school teachers and Bible study leaders in my
church. May they enjoy bold access into Your

*I*n whom we have boldness and access with confidence through faith in Him.

EPHESIANS 3:12, NKJV

presence day by day and refreshment from Your Word. Empower them, by Your Spirit, in their personal and family lives and in their teaching and leading. Help them realize that their work as Your servants is Your work. Enable them to surrender their service into Your hands and let You work in them and through them.

May the classes attract newcomers and draw them back week after week. Use these ministries to bring many to Christ and ground them in You and in Your Word. Use them to prepare people who, in turn, will become teachers and leaders, in both the near and distant future.

I pray these same requests for Sunday schools and Bible studies throughout our area—and beyond.

Scripture References (by paragraph)

1. Hebrews 4:16
2. Ephesians 3:12; 2 Peter 1:3–4; Psalm 1:2–3; Zechariah 4:6; Proverbs 16:3; Hebrews 13:20–21; Psalm 115:1

As You Have Time

A CONFIDENT APPROACH. "Let us...approach the throne of grace with confidence" (Hebrews 4:16, NIV). Why can we come with confidence? Is it because we're worthy, or skilled in prayer? No. It's because Jesus, our great High Priest, who understands us and sympathizes with our weaknesses, invites us to come boldly (Hebrews 4:16; Ephesians 3:12). So if you feel inadequate in prayer, don't get discouraged and stop praying. "We learn to pray by praying." Keep on praying, coming to God simply yet confidently, as a small child comes to his father. Count on the Lord to teach you to pray. He's an excellent Tutor.

INCREASING YOUR BOLDNESS. The Bible contains many prayers, many promises, many snapshots of our God of goodness and power. As you are able to imprint these in your memory and spirit, you will become increasingly bold in your faith. Copy favorite passages on cards or in a notebook, and use them in prayer.

You can also increase your boldness and confidence through praise, especially when you ground your praise in God's Word. The praise part of today's prayer, for example, was based on Hebrews 4:16.

PRAY FOR HOLINESS.

Holy Father, thank You that we are Your chosen ones, holy in Your sight and deeply loved. How wonderful that, by sacrificing Your Son, You have perfected us in our inmost being.

Now, Lord, enable me to live out what You have done deep within me. How much I need greater holiness! May Your Spirit of holiness empower me to grow in righteous thinking and living.

I pray this also for believers in my neighborhood and church—and for others who come to mind:

Make us quick to confess our sins and rely on You to forgive. Make us clean and pure in every part of our lives. Deliver us from the evil ways we used to cherish when we didn't know any better. May we feed daily on Your holy Scriptures, letting You use them to cleanse our lives and remove our blemishes and wrinkles and defects.

*D*ear brothers and sisters, you are foreigners and aliens here. So I warn you to keep away from evil desires because they fight against your very souls.

1 PETER 2:11, NLT

I pray that Your people—and especially the Christians I know—will grow in holiness so that we will not dishonor Your name by compromised living. May we be blameless and contagious Christians, a good advertisement for the gospel.

I worship before You as the God of peace and well-being who is committed to making us holy. I count on You to do this day by day, giving us grace to cooperate with You. How I rejoice that You are faithful. You will continue Your work in us until the day when You bring us faultless into Your glorious presence, with unspeakable joy.

Scripture References (by paragraph)

1. Colossians 3:12; Hebrews 10:14
2. Philippians 2:12–13; Luke 1:74–75; Isaiah 48:17–18
3. 1 Thessalonians 5:23; 1 Peter 1:14–15; 1 John 1:9; Ephesians 5:26–27
4. Titus 2:10
5. 1 Thessalonians 5:24; Leviticus 20:8; Jude 1:24

As You Have Time

THE HARD, PLEASANT WORK OF PRAYER. "To a healthy man work that interests him is a pleasure; he brings enormous energy to it. In the same way, the believer who is in full spiritual health will pray diligently." Andrew Murray

GROWING IN HOLINESS AND FAITH. How do we increase our holiness and our faith? By pursuing a deeper knowledge of God. Every truth we grasp about Him increases our level of confidence in Him and makes us more like Him. So let's pursue Him diligently—"Let us press on to know the LORD" (Hosea 6:3). "He rewards those who earnestly seek him" (Hebrews 11:6, NIV). George Mueller wrote, "Let no man think he can have any measure of victory over his inner corruption without taking it to the Lord again and again in prayer." The same holds true in praying for other believers.

> I want a principle within
> Of watchful, godly fear,
> A sensitivity to sin,
> A pain to feel it near.
> Help me the first approach to feel
> Of pride or wrong desire,
> To catch the wandering of the will
> And quench the kindling fire.

CHARLES WESLEY

For more help, see "Count on the Truth of Instant Forgiveness," page 181.

PRAY FOR THE CHURCH OF THE
FUTURE, FOR THE GENERATION
NOW GROWING UP.

Father, You are God throughout all
generations, and You are deeply concerned
about the temptations and moral pressures young
people face today. I lift to You the young in my
church, in my family and neighborhood, and
beyond.

Draw them to Christ, and to true freedom
through knowing and obeying Your Word. May they
see You as good and desirable and loving; may they
learn to love You with all their hearts and trust Your
good plan for their futures. Give them godly role
models and strong biblical convictions.

Give fathers and mothers great wisdom in
bringing them up with loving discipline, Bible-
centered instruction, and much prayer. And give
children grace to love, respect, and obey their
parents. May the parents be good examples in their
walk with You and their love for each other. Work

I will pour out my Spirit on your offspring,
and my blessing on your descendants.

ISAIAH 44:3, NIV

mightily to overcome problems in marriages and to keep the parents together. And give special grace and help to families with only one parent.

Guide parents in their decisions about their children's education. Even when situations and educational opportunities are far from ideal—as with Samuel and Daniel, who were surrounded by evil—enable parents to lay strong spiritual foundations in each child's life.

Protect students from being misled by peer pressure and by the world's ways of thinking and living.

Encourage and strengthen Christian teachers in their important work. And I pray for all who minister to children, students, and families. May Your Spirit deeply touch many lives through them. I especially lift up _____, _____, and _____, asking for wisdom, strength, and encouragement for them.

Scripture References (by paragraph)

1. Psalm 90:1–2; Matthew 6:13
2. John 6:44; 8:31–32; Luke 10:27; Jeremiah 29:11;
   Psalm 34:10; Proverbs 13:20
3. Ephesians 6:4; 6:1–2; Deuteronomy 6:6–7
4. Matthew 7:24–25; I Samuel 1:22; 2:11–12, 17, 22; Daniel 1:3–8;
   Proverbs 1:10, 15–16, 23; Colossians 2:8

As You Have Time

GUARDIANS OF THE YOUNG. Select and pray for a few
organizations that work with children, young
people, and students. Pray that God will thwart
influences of our age that especially concern you—
drugs, pornography, sexual permissiveness and
abuse, damaging music, negative influences through
the media and through some school districts and
colleges.

THE LANGUAGE OF A PARENT'S LONGING. Amy
Carmichael founded the Dohnavur Fellowship in
India for desperately needy children. She wrote a

touching prayer for her many children, beseeching the Father to bring them safely through life's troubled waters. "Read the language of our longing...Holy Father, for our children," she pleaded. "And wherever they may bide, lead them Home at eventide."

In a similar vein, Lamentations 2:19 says, "Arise, cry out in the night...pour out your heart like water in the presence of the Lord.... For the lives of your children" (NIV).

Build your personal collection of Bible verses to use in prayer for young people. As a start, meditate on the following and apply them to the children and teenagers you pray for: Luke 2:52; Psalm 90:14, 16; 119:9–11, 18; 143:8–10. And let God use Isaiah 49:25 to urge you to pray for children in these troubled and perilous times.

PRAY FOR GRACE TO BE
DILIGENT IN PRAYER.

It's a pleasure, Lord, to come into Your presence, and be still before You, and rest in Your love. How good it is to worship You and commune with You. And what strength and refreshment come from warm fellowship with You!

But don't let me forget that prayer is more than this. Give me grace to work diligently in prayer for others. And as You lead, to wrestle earnestly in prayer on their behalf. Put special burdens on my heart, and enable me to pour out my heart for You to fulfill Your purposes.

Father, Your great desire is for all Your children to be both mature and effective. Do this for me, and for those in my church. Do it for fellow believers throughout our area. And our country. Do it for all believers!

Thank You for Your Spirit and the power He gives me to serve You—and others—through prayer.

*E*paphras, who is one of you...is always wrestling in prayer for you, that you may stand firm in all the will of God, mature and fully assured.

COLOSSIANS 4:12, NIV

Thank You for the way praise refreshes and strengthens me to work hard in prayer, and the way it stimulates my faith and helps assure answers.

Greatly use those who are seeking to rally Your people to pray. Raise up many who will pray faithfully, pleading with You to work mightily in all the world.

Scripture References (by paragraph)

1. Psalm 46:10; 23:2; 116:7; Numbers 6:24–26; Matthew 11:28–29; John 14:27; 2 Corinthians 4:16
2. Colossians 4:12; 2:1–2; Ephesians 6:12, 18
3. Ephesians 4:14–16; 2 Peter 1:2–8; 3:18
4. Acts 3:19; 2 Chronicles 20:20–22

AS YOU HAVE TIME

OUR UNLIMITED GOD. "'He did not do many miracles there because of their lack of faith' (Matthew 13:58).

Beware, above everything else in your praying, of limiting God, not only by unbelief but also by fancying that you know what He can do. Expect unexpected things, 'abundantly above all that we ask or think' (Ephesians 3:20). Each time you intercede, be quiet first and worship God in His glory. Meditate on what He can do. Then expect great things!" Andrew Murray

PRAY BIG AND BROADLY. Thank the Lord often that He is able to do far beyond your highest prayers and thoughts.

> You are coming to a King,
> Large petitions with you bring;
> For His grace and power are such,
> None can ever ask too much.

AUTHOR UNKNOWN

We have personally profited from Andrew Murray's emphasis on praying for groups of people—even "all believers" and "all people." Paul wrote, "Be persistent in your prayers for all Christians everywhere.... I urge you...to pray for all people" (Ephesians 6:18; 1 Timothy 2:1, NLT). We've found it refreshing to do more of this broad praying while not neglecting pointed prayers for specific people.

PRAY FOR GOD'S PURIFYING

WORK.

Holy Father, Holy Son, Holy Spirit—God of awesome holiness and purity, of power and righteous judgment! I stand in awe of You, in holy dread of disobeying You, for You are a blazing, purifying fire. I also thank You that You are eager to consume everything that detracts from my well-being, my relationships, and my nearness to You.

"Who of us can dwell with the consuming fire? He who walks righteously...." Lord, I long to live righteously every day, all day long. How much I need Your purifying presence to reprove me and purge my life of all that grieves You. Many of Your people likewise need refining fires to reveal and burn out sin. Bring release from the things that bind us—compromise, complacency, tolerance of sin, materialism, love of power, infighting, gossip, lack of spiritual depth. Give each of us a spirit of repentance and power to live our lives with reverent

The Lord...will cleanse...by a spirit of judgment and a spirit of fire.

ISAIAH 4:4, NIV

fear of You. Implant deep within me a hatred for sin and an enduring longing to be more like You.

Thank You, Father, that You discipline me because You want to adorn my character with the purity and beauty of Christ. Enable me to trust Your loving intentions and not to resist You. When You, as a refiner of silver, use painful, fiery trials to bring the scum to the top in my life, give me grace to cooperate with You in removing it rather than just stirring it back in.

I praise You that You are full of compassion and that the outcome of Your purifying work is more than worth all You let us go through.

Scripture References (by paragraph)

1. Psalm 99:1–3; Revelation 15:4; Isaiah 6:3, 5;
   1 Peter 1:16–17; Hebrews. 12:29
2. Isaiah 33:14–15; Malachi 3:3; Proverbs 8:18
3. Hebrews 12:7–11; Isaiah 48:10;
   Romans 5:3–4; 1 Peter 1:7
4. 1 Thessalonians 5:18; James 5:11

As You Have Time

A CLEAN HEART. "Our power to bless others and to intercede successfully can only flourish as sins are faced and put away. Sanctification begins with a troubling awareness of our own sin. Plead with God today for a 'spirit of fire' to uncover and burn out sin in His people, so that they will be blessed and become a blessing to the world." Andrew Murray

THE GOLD IN TRIALS. How often in our trials our plea is "Lord, quick! Change my situation! Make my life easier!" But His love is set on changing us, on bringing us forth as gold (Job 23:10). Instead of pleading for fast relief, we find it helpful to pray, "Father, change me! Don't end this trial until You've done all You want to do in my life through it." This is not a noble prayer, but simply a sensible one. Who wants added trials to accomplish what God intends to do in the present trial? Pray along with the sentiments of this unknown author:

> Purge me, Lord, of my follies,
> An empty cup let me be
> Waiting only Thy blessing,
> Hungry only for Thee.
>
> Can even the Lord pour blessing
> Into a cup that is full?
> Put treasure into a locked hand
> Be He ever so bountiful?
>
> Empty me, Lord, and make me
> Hungry only for Thee.
> Only Thy bread, once tasted,
> Can ever satisfy me.

PRAY FOR LOVE IN THE
CHURCH.

Dear Father, the Source of every mercy, how I
thank You that each of Your children is dear
to You—as dear as Your beloved Son!

You love us, even though we differ in some of
our doctrines and spiritual practices. You still love us
even when we sin! Lord, how unworthy I am of such
love! How unworthy we all are! And how much we
need to grow in loving others as You love us!

Enable each of us—in my church and in all
churches everywhere—to experience Your love
more fully, and to let it flow out to others. May Your
Spirit fill us day by day, bringing forth the fresh,
abundant fruit of love in our lives. Love that keeps
growing richer in knowledge and wise insight, in
patience and kindness, in humility that honors the
other person. Love that overcomes jealousy and
arrogance and self-seeking. Love that is not touchy
or resentful or judgmental. Love that covers a

*B*e joyful always; pray continually; give thanks in all circumstances, for this is God's will for you.

1 THESSALONIANS 5:16–18, NIV

multitude of sins and refuses to gossip. Love that chooses to look out for the other person's interests, as well as our own—whether we feel like it or not. Work in me this kind of love for all believers—and especially for those I find hard to love and those who tend to rub me the wrong way.

May we constantly show the fragrant love of Christ to one another, as we look forward to being together for all eternity. May the world see Your love in our lives, and may this draw many to You.

Scripture References (by paragraph)

1. John 17:23
2. Hosea 3:1; Luke 15:11–24
3. John 13:34–35; Galatians 5:22; Philippians 1:9;
   1 Corinthians 13:4–7; 1 Peter 4:8; Philippians 2:3–4
4. Ephesians 5:1–2; John 13:34

As You Have Time

PRAY ALONG WITH SCRIPTURE. Praying God's Word makes for powerful praying. Follow Paul's prayer in Ephesians 3:17–19, NLT: Pray that believers' roots (including yours) will go deep into the soil of God's marvelous love, and that they will have the power to understand how wide, how long, how high, and how deep His love really is and to experience this love for themselves.

Then pray for the outshining of this love, based on Ephesians 4:2–3, NLT: Pray that believers—those the Lord brings to mind as well as yourself—will be humble and gentle, patient with each other, making allowances for each other's faults because of their love; that they will keep themselves united in the Holy Spirit and bound together in peace.

FEELINGS IN CONFLICT. Praying only when we feel like praying greatly hinders faithful and continual prayer. So refuse to let conflicting feelings and interests keep you from prayer. Say yes to prayer by saying no to other things you feel like doing or feel pressed to do. And pray often that your feelings will learn to cooperate. Ask the Lord to stir your heart to pray, both in your set times of prayer and in on-the-spot praying.

For more help, see "Depend on the Word, Not Feelings," page 193.

PRAY FOR THE WORLD'S PEOPLES
WHO ARE STILL IN DARKNESS.

Father, how wonderful to be a child of the
great King over all the earth—a God of love
who does not want anyone to perish but wants
everyone to come to repentance, to freedom, and to
fullness of life. I worship You!

Thank You that my prayers can help fulfill
Your longings to include in Your family people from
every tribe and language and people and nation.
What a family to belong to! And what an honor to
help in this tremendous task through prayer!

Yet how terrible is the destiny of those who
ignore Your salvation! Stir my heart, Lord—and the
hearts of countless others—to pray more for those
who have heard of You but have not yet responded.
And for the millions who are still without the
gospel.

Lord, You are the Master of breakthroughs.
Bring mighty breakthroughs of the gospel

*T*he Lord…is patient with you, not wanting anyone to perish but everyone to come to repentance.

2   PETER   3:9,   NIV

throughout the world. Penetrate Satan's lines of defense. Do this especially among Muslims, among Buddhists, among Hindus, among Jews, as well as among atheists—these great strongholds that the gospel has barely dented. Break through, Lord, to their leaders and to their people. May the reality of Christ and His saving love dawn in their hearts like a brilliant sunrise. And may Your Spirit work with unusual power through those who are ministering among them.

You have promised that the ends of the earth will be Your Son's possession. I ask You to accomplish this soon.

Scripture References (by paragraph)

1. Psalm 47:2; 2 Peter 3:9
2. Revelation 5:9–10
3. 2 Thessalonians 1:8–10; Revelation 21:8
4. 2 Samuel 5:20, note in NASB margin; Isaiah 9:2; 2 Corinthians 4:6
5. Psalm 2:8

As You Have Time

URGENT PRAYER NEEDED! Think of the world's 6 billion people and how many die each year without receiving Christ. (In India, 800 million are still submerged in Hinduism; in China alone, 2 million die every month without Christ). Pour out your heart to God for them.

And don't forget the Jews and all the ministries to Jews around the world. Consider God's heart for the Jewish people throughout the centuries, though most have spurned His Son, His best love gift to them. He expressed His love so well in Hosea 11:8, NLT: "O how can I give you up, Israel? How can I let You go? How can I destroy you...? My heart is torn within me, and my compassion overflows." Your prayers can hasten the day when God will restore the nation of Israel to Himself and to His great purposes for them.

J. O. Fraser wrote: "Many of us cannot reach the mission fields on our feet, but we can reach them on our knees. Solid, lasting missionary work is accomplished by prayer, whether offered in China, India or the United States."

PRAY FOR ALL WHO PROFESS TO
BE CHRISTIANS.

O my Strength, I will sing praise to You, for You, my loving God, are my strength, my fortress, my joy, my reward. I rejoice again in Your unlimited power and Your many promises to answer prayer. My heart trusts You, and I am helped and deeply blessed.

Lord, how Your heart is grieved by the many people who seem to be Christians in name only—by the more than 1 billion nominal Christians in the world today. Have mercy on them—including the ones I know personally. Whether they are lukewarm believers or don't know You at all, convince them of their sins and spiritual sicknesses, their empty ritualism, their compromise, their ignorance and indifference, their loving what gives them pleasure rather than loving You. Help them see that they have a mere form of godliness without the content.

Be gracious to them, Lord, so that in the end

$\mathcal{T}$ruly my soul silently waits for God.

PSALM 62:1, NKJV

they will not lose everything they've lived for and receive no rewards. And draw those who don't know You to Your Son so that in the end He will not have to say, "I never knew You; depart from Me for your deeds are evil."

Thank You, Father, for Your heart of compassion toward these people, though You hate their ways. I plead with You to work in their lives. Make them aware of Your deep longing to make them truly—and wholly—Yours. Deliver them from merely acting as if they know You. Bring them into true faith and a full commitment to Christ. Lead them into a warm, vital relationship with You. May Your Spirit work in their lives—and mine—with mighty power, making us a glory to Your name.

Today, I pray these requests especially for

_____.

Scripture References (by paragraph)

1. Psalm 59:16–17; 43:4; Genesis 15:1; Jeremiah. 32:17;
   Psalm 28:7
2. 2 Timothy 3:2–5
3. 1 Corinthians 3:15
4. Matthew 6:21–23

As You Have Time

BE STILL AND KNOW. Andrew Murray wrote, "The nearer we come to God Himself and the deeper we enter into His will, the more power we have in prayer. In the stillness you will receive power to pray." (For more help, see "Learn to Be Still before God," page 197.)

Here's a prayer to use as you pursue a deeper knowledge of God and richer times of stillness in His presence:

Dear Father, how I long to know You better. Reveal Yourself to me in new ways as I wait quietly before You. Make Yourself more real to me than anyone or anything on earth. Open my eyes to see You in the Scriptures; quiet my mind and emotions to be still and know that You are God. Calm my heart, taking away my strain and stress. Make me conscious of Your presence as I wait before You with holy reverence.

2 PETER 1:2–4; PSALM 73:25–26;
PROVERBS 2:1–5; PSALM 46:10

Lord Jesus, make Yourself to me
A living, bright reality,
More present to faith's vision keen
Than any earthly object seen;
More dear, more intimately nigh
Than e'en the sweetest earthly tie.

HUDSON TAYLOR

PRAY FOR NEW BELIEVERS.

Dear Lord, thank You for inviting me to join this strategic ministry of intercession. Show me which persons You most want me to pray for, and help me pray for them often, without giving up.

Thank You, Father, for Your tender heart toward the newly born-again children in Your family. How grieved You are when they remain weak infants or become lukewarm or fall into sin. Protect and encourage the new family members I know, and others around the world, especially _____ and _____. Give special grace and deliverance to those strongly surrounded by Satan's power. Deliver them from the evil one.

Assure new believers of their salvation and give them a hunger for the spiritual milk of Your Word. Help them pray and not lose heart. Lead them to nurturing groups of believers where Your Word is

*A*s newborn babes, desire the pure milk of the word, that you may grow thereby.

1 PETER 2:2, NKJV

proclaimed and where older Christians will help them grow.

Teach them the wonder of Christ's presence within them and how fully they belong to You. Fill their hearts with thankfulness and with glad surrender.

Scripture References (by paragraph)

1. Ephesians 6:18; 1 Timothy 2:1, 3
2. Isaiah 40:11; Ephesians 4:14; Matthew 6:13
3. 1 John 5:13; 1 Peter 2:2–3; Romans 12:2; Luke 18:1; Ephesians 4:15; Hebrews 10:24–25
4. Colossians 1:27; 1 Corinthians 6:19–20; Romans 14:7–9; Ephesians 1:3; Romans 12:1

AS YOU HAVE TIME

THE TONIC OF WORSHIP. In *Praise: A Door to God's Presence,* we wrote about the benefits of praise-filled praying: "God places great importance on worship, praise, and thanksgiving. He does so not because He is an egoist with selfish desires, but because He has our best interests at heart. Praise and thanksgiving help us rise above self-centeredness to Christ-centeredness. They focus our hearts and minds on the Lord and make us more like Him. We cheat ourselves when we neglect them, for they are a tonic that promotes joy and spiritual vigor."

The Bible sparkles with praise passages that express in inspired words the wonders of our God. Some Old Testament favorites: 1 Chronicles 16:27–29; 29:11–12; Psalm 68:32–35; 73:25–26; 84:11–12; 90:1–2; 93:3–4; 103:1–5; 145:8–9; Isaiah 25:1; 40:12–13; 64:4; Jeremiah 10:6–7, 10; 32:17; Lamentations 3:22–24.

CHANGE OF PACE. Try using photographs or a map of the world to prompt your prayers.

Occasionally pray for people, places, and needs far outside your usual range of concerns. Or carry your day's requests around with you on a slip of paper to use in spare moments or on a prayer walk.

PRAY FOR PASTORS.

Father, how much I praise You for our Lord
Jesus, the good Shepherd who knows His
sheep and laid down His life for us. Thank You for
the gracious way He ministers to our needs day by
day. And for the millions of pastors You have raised
up throughout the world to help Him in His
shepherding.

I plead with You for my pastor and other
ministers, priests, and spiritual caregivers in our area.
Empower them day by day to shepherd Your flock
under their care. May they "set an example for the
believers in speech, in life, in love, in faith, and in
purity."

Give them grace in the trials and temptations
so many of them face: few words of appreciation,
much criticism, excessive demands on their time,
the difficulty of saying no, sexual temptations,
financial stresses and temptations, fear of man,

"Far be it from me that I should sin against the LORD by ceasing to pray for you."

1 SAMUEL 12:23

trying to please everyone, the danger of feeling they're always right, and self-dependence, to name a few.

Motivate them to press on to know You better, spending much time in Your Word and in prayer. May they teach not human wisdom but Your wisdom. May they rely on You and Your sufficiency rather than their own.

Grant them wisdom in the complexities of their work and in equipping their people to use their gifts and carry their share of the ministry. In all things may they seek Your glory and not their own.

And, Lord, do these same things for the multitude of pastors in Your worldwide church— and for other leaders and teachers in each of Your churches, including mine.

Scripture References (by paragraph)

1. John 10:11; Psalm 23:1
2. 2 Timothy 1:7; 1 Peter 5:2–3; 1 Timothy 4:12
3. Matthew 6:13; 1 Corinthians 10:13
4. Hosea 6:3; 1 Corinthians 2:6–7, 11–13;
   Deuteronomy 32:2–3; 2 Corinthians 3:5
5. Ephesians 4:11–12; Romans 12:4–8;
   2 Timothy 2:1–2

As You Have Time

SPECIAL NEEDS OF PASTORS AND THEIR SPOUSES. For
those pastors who have families, ask the Lord to
enable them to fulfill their God-given roles as
husbands and fathers, taking time to love and bless
their wives and children as well as their flock. And
pray for their children. It's not easy to be a
"preacher's kid" (Titus 2:3–5; Ephesians 5:25–31; 6:4;
Colossians 3:18–22).

Pastors' wives also face challenging circumstances
and many impossible expectations. Pray for them!

Lord, thank You for our pastor's wife and her highly important role. May she enjoy a rich personal walk with You day by day; may she let You meet her deepest needs. Keep her looking to You for strength and wisdom, including wisdom in what she says and repeats. Help her be faithful in prayer for her husband, especially for the specific needs she knows better than anyone else. I ask the same, Lord, for other pastors' wives, nearby and around the world, such as _____, _____, and _____.

Easy-to-remember times to pray regularly for pastors are on Saturday as you think about the coming Lord's Day and on your way to church.

PRAY FOR GOD'S POWER ON ALL
WHO SERVE THE LORD—
LAY AND FULL-TIME.

Gracious Father, thank You for raising up
full-time ministers and laymen and
laywomen to serve You in a wide variety of
ministries. I especially thank You for _____
and _____. Bless them in every area of their
lives. In their physical, emotional, and spiritual
health. In their marriages and families and other
relationships. In their finances and paperwork. In
their personal struggles and temptations. In their
time pressures. In their recreation.

May all Your servants take time daily to seek
You earnestly in Your Word and in prayer, refusing
to let busyness and distractions squeeze You out.
Give them wisdom in what to say yes to and no to—
even in ministry opportunities. Give the laypeople
special wisdom in juggling the demands of their
jobs, families, and ministries.

*Y*ou help us by your prayers.

2 C O R I N T H I A N S 1 : 1 1 , N I V

May those who serve You be strong in Your
grace to disciple and coach younger Christians, to
endure hardships, and to steer clear of needless
entanglements. May they see Your Spirit work
powerfully in their ministries.

Scripture References (by paragraph)

1. Numbers 6:24–26; Psalm 67:1; 1 Chronicles 4:10
2. Psalm 1:2–3; Jeremiah. 29:13; Luke 10:41–42
3. 2 Timothy 2:1–4; Psalm 90:16–17

AS YOU HAVE TIME

PARTNERING WITH SPECIFIC MINISTRIES. "Be specific in your
petitions," wrote Andrew Murray, "then you'll know
what answers to look for. Intercession is not the
breathing out of pious wishes; its aim is to bring down
God's blessing through believing, persevering prayer."

Be receptive to focusing prayer on specific
ministries the Lord lays on your heart. Consider

some possibilities: ministries in our military services, in inner cities, in isolated rural areas, and in special ethnic groups; ministries to the sick, the poor, the physically and mentally disabled, prisoners, drug addicts, unwed mothers; ministries in publications, Christian radio, and TV.

ENRICHING AND EXPANDING YOUR INTERCESSION. As you spend time in God's Word, be on the watch for passages that relate to any of the thirty-one days, and copy them for monthly use. Some Scriptures that may help you pray for people serving the Lord are 2 Corinthians 2:10; 3:5, 17–18 and Ephesians 6:19–20. Or glean requests from chapters such as 2 Corinthians 4 or Romans 8.

Always remember that those in special ministries—no matter how spiritually gifted they may seem—are as human as you are. Start with the same requests you pray for yourself!

PRAY FOR MORE WORKERS IN
GOD'S HARVEST.

Sovereign Lord—head of the Church,
commander of Your armies, Lord of the
harvest—You know the need for workers in our
country and throughout the world. Give me, and
other intercessors, diligence in praying for more
workers.

I plead with You to raise up mature and
effective men and women and young people and
send them out from our church, our Sunday school,
and our youth group. Do the same in other churches
in our country and in other parts of the world.

I pray for the people You plan to send—some
of them now students in seminaries, Bible schools,
and other training programs. Teach them to abide in
Christ and to nourish their souls in Your Word.
Empower them by Your Spirit to reap and build
right where they are, and make them ready to go
wherever You send them—some into needy areas

"The harvest is plentiful but the workers are few. Ask the Lord of the harvest, therefore, to send out workers into his harvest field."

MATTHEW 9:37–38, NIV

and closed countries where people live in deep darkness.

Work in all Your people, Lord. Make us willing to follow You anywhere, anytime, with or without anybody or anything but You. Wherever You lead us, may our primary interest be the things that are on Your heart.

Scripture References (by paragraph)

1. —
2. Ephesians 1:22; Joshua 5:14; Matthew 9:38
3. John 15:5; Acts 20:32; Joshua 1:8; Acts 1:8; Matthew 28:20
4. John 12:25–26; Luke 9:23; Matthew 6:33

As You Have Time

USE GOD'S WORD IN PRAYER. For richer and more powerful praying, weave Scriptures into your prayers. This will strengthen your faith, focus your heart and mind, and keep you praying according to the will of God. As Andrew Murray wrote, "God's listening to our voice depends upon our listening to His voice.... Our whole life must be under the supremacy of the Word: the Word must be dwelling in us."

Use verses that the Holy Spirit brings to your attention in your quiet time and verses you have memorized. Search out prayers and benedictions in the Bible. We've listed below some references to get you started. Select the ones that mean the most to you and copy them for easy use. Then as you're able, meditate more deeply on each one. Use them in prayer often, for yourself and others.

Some prayers and benedictions: Numbers 6:24–26; 1 Chronicles 4:10; Psalm 25:4–5; 57:1–2; 119:9–11, 73; 143:8–10; Ephesians 1:17–21; 3:16–21; Philippians 1:9–11; Colossians 1:9–12;

1 Thessalonians 5:23–24; 2 Thessalonians 2:16–17; 3:16; Hebrews 13:20–21.

Other great passages for prayer: Psalm 84:11–12; Isaiah 55:1–3; Habakkuk 3:17; Romans 5:1–5; 8:1–4; 31–39; Ephesians 1:3–13; Philippians 3:7–10; Colossians 3:1–17; Hebrews 12:1–2; 2 Peter 1:2–8.

PRAY FOR WORLDWIDE
MISSIONS.

Father, give Your people hearts that burn with
Your longing for the Good News to be
preached throughout the world, and begin this work
in my heart. May we desire what You so deeply
desire to do—to bring people into Your family and
mold them into the image of Christ. May we
faithfully invest our prayers, our time, and our
money in what is on Your heart.

Bring a revival of urgent prayer among all Your
people. May more churches, everywhere in the
world, become missions-minded. May they send out
people who are close to You, empowered by You,
and equipped to serve and pray effectively.

Show me, Lord, which mission groups and
which parts of the world—which cities, countries, or
people groups—You most want me to pray for. And
enable me to pray with a growing faith, confident
that my prayers indeed make a difference in the

*"*And this gospel of the kingdom will be preached in the whole world as a testimony to all nations, and then the end will come.... Go into all the world and preach the good news to all creation."*

MATTHEW 24:14; MARK 16:15, NIV

world, removing mountains that hinder Your work and bringing about impossible things.

Lord, You're in charge of the harvest. Cause countless people to turn from darkness to light and from the power of Satan to You. Do this in every tribe, every language, and every religion—even in the most hard-to-reach places and the most resistant religions.

Lord, these are big requests but not too big for You!

Scripture References (by paragraph)

1. Matthew 28:19–20; Acts 15:14; Romans 8:29
2. —
3. Mark 11:22–24; Matthew 17:20; Luke 1:37; 18:27
4. Acts 26:18; Revelation 5:9

As You Have Time

THE SIZE OF THE TASK. In view of how much our fallen world needs continual prayer—and how inadequate our praying time seems—consider some ways to match need with practice:

- We can tailor our prayer life to fit each stage of our earthly life and spiritual growth, beginning with ten or fifteen minutes, then letting the time grow.
- We can learn to pray more throughout the day. Continual praying is not something we suddenly decide to do. It's something we grow into.

For more help, see "View Prayer As a Way of Life," page 202.

WORLDWIDE TEAMS ALREADY AT WORK. Pray that God's Spirit will work mightily through the many round-the-world ministries He has raised up. Ask Him to guide you to several missionary societies or projects with which you can partner in prayer.

S. D. Gordon gave this encouragement:

> Prayer puts us into direct dynamic touch with a world. A man may go aside today, and shut his door, and as truly spend a half-hour in India for God as though he were there in person.... Surely you and I must get more half-hours for this secret service.

PRAY FOR GOD'S BLESSING
ON OUR MISSIONARIES.

Dear Lord, Your eyes are searching the whole earth to strengthen those who are fully committed to You. May Your missionaries be fully committed today, and give them strength equal to the work You have assigned them. Enable them to stand firm against the schemes of the devil. I pray this especially for those laboring in Satan's strongholds where his power has scarcely been challenged. And I want to include in these requests some missionaries I know: _____ .

May they cultivate a strong and fresh grasp on Your Word—the sword of Your Spirit. Increasingly make them men and women of prayer. Protect them from getting swamped by demands that crowd out time alone with You.

May they rejoice in Your sufficiency and rely on You for wisdom and peace. Grant love and harmony in how they relate to their partners and children, to

*"*__B__*ut* you will receive power when the Holy Spirit comes on you; and you will be my witnesses...to the ends of the earth."

other missionaries, and to the people they work among. You know their personal trials today—loneliness, homesickness, the need for patience, official red tape, struggles in language learning, on and on. Give them grace to trust You as their refuge and strength, as their sun and shield, as the best Person in their lives.

Put Your full blessing on their evangelism, their discipling, their church responsibilities—and on those with other gifts and callings. In the name of Jesus, the mighty Victor, defeat Satan's attempts to blind people to the gospel and prevent the growth of believers.

Scripture References (by paragraph)

1. 2 Chronicles 16:8–9; Deuteronomy 33:25;
   Ephesians 6:10–11
2. Ephesians 6:17–18; Luke 10:39–42
3. 2 Corinthians 3:4–6; Ephesians 4:2–3;
   Psalm 46:1; 84:11; 73:25–26
4. Psalm 67:1–2; Colossians 4:3–4;
   2 Corinthians 4:4; 1 Peter 5:8–9

148   THIRTY-ONE DAYS OF PRAYER

As You Have Time

"HE DID NOT STAGGER..." As you intercede, count on God's faithfulness to His promises. Be like Abraham, who the Bible says "did not stagger" (lose confidence; flounder in confusion, doubt, or uncertainty) even though God's plan seemed humanly impossible. Instead, Abraham was absolutely convinced that God was able to do anything He promised.

Read I Kings 8:56; Romans 4:20–21; and Hebrews 11:8–19, and start your collection of prayer promises.

ORDINARY STRAINS, EXTRAORDINARY SITUATIONS. Many difficulties your missionaries face don't differ from those you face in your family, church, work, health, finances, or emotional struggles. But added stress comes through dealing with these difficulties in a foreign land and culture. These pressures are often greatest for wives and single women, who need to grapple more with the nitty-gritty of daily living. Identify with missionaries as ordinary people, not as spiritual giants unaffected by trials. Then you'll know better how to pray.

Your prayers sustain overseas Christian workers. A newsletter from friends working in a difficult country put it well: "We ran out of emotional energy and felt we just couldn't handle any more. If people back home stop praying, we're not going to make it."

PRAY FOR ALL WHO ARE
SUFFERING.

Father, I rejoice in You as the Father of deep
empathies, who comforts and encourages us. I
need this so often, and so do millions of others in
Your family and outside. How little I really feel the
wrenching sorrows and hopelessness of people as
You do. Stir my heart, Lord. In new ways make
me—and all Your children—channels of Your love
and compassion, spending ourselves in both prayer
and action for those who suffer.

Lord, help those who are suffering. Again and
again meet their needs—physical, financial,
emotional, spiritual. Through their pain or loss or
trouble, make them aware of how much they need
You. Then draw them to You as their Savior and
Shepherd—and their Lord. Comfort them in their
anguish, their pain, their depression, their despair.
Deliver them.

I pray especially for Your people who are going

$\mathcal{T}$he God and Father of our Lord Jesus Christ, the Father of compassion...comforts us in all our troubles.

2 CORINTHIANS 1:3-4, NIV

through intense persecution, torture, imprisonment. Help them and their families lean hard on You, and give them supernatural strength. Protect them, encourage them, and uphold them. Provide for their every need. Make Your presence unspeakably real to them.

Give Your joy to those who suffer. Put a new song of praise in their mouth, so that many will hear what You've done and put their trust in You.

Scripture References (by paragraph)

1. 2 Corinthians 1:3–4; Isaiah 58:10–11
2. Isaiah 63:9; 2 Thessalonians 2:16–17; 3:16
3. Isaiah 41:10; 43:2
4. Isaiah 61:1–3; Psalm 40:3

AS YOU HAVE TIME

TARGETING TROUBLE. Pray for one or two areas of suffering that seem to be particularly intense or ongoing. Daily headlines can serve as a reminder. Some prompters on this long, dismaying list include: wars, atrocities, refugees, famines, terror and hate crimes, satanism, poverty, drug addiction, abused wives and children, children and teens living on the streets.

Be encouraged to continue in this serious work of prayer by Charles Spurgeon's words:

> It is good that we are commanded to pray, or else in times of heaviness we might give it up. If God commands me, unfit as I may be, I will creep to the footstool of grace; and since He says, "Pray without ceasing," though my words fail me and my heart itself will wander, yet I will still stammer out the wishes of my hungering soul and say, "O God, at least teach me to pray and help me to prevail with You."

ARROW PRAYERS. When Ruth hears of an urgent need, she prays when the news comes or as soon afterward as possible. Then as she goes about her day, she continues to release quick "arrow" prayers: "Lord, work! Work mightily!" Or, "Lord, meet their needs!" Or, "Lord, I'm believing You to answer." These simple, urgent petitions strengthen her faith and keep her praying even if she's extra busy.

PRAY FOR PRESIDENTS,
PRIME MINISTERS, AND ALL
IN AUTHORITY.

Father, how privileged I am to be able to pray
to You! You are God Most High, ruler over
the kingdoms of the world, infinitely greater than all
earthly authorities. Nations are as nothing in Your
sight—like a drop in a bucket. And You reduce
political leaders to nothing by merely blowing on
them. What a mighty God You are!

To think that You have decreed that our prayers
actually influence what You do! And that You are
alert day and night, ready to listen to our requests!

I praise You that the hearts of earthly rulers
are like streams of water that You direct as You
please. Bring about wise decisions in the
government and courts of our country.

For the good of Your people and for the spread
of the gospel, overrule bad decisions, mistakes, and
evil plans. Do the same for all city and state
governments, for leaders of other countries, and for

$\mathcal{I}$ urge, then...that requests, prayers, intercession and thanksgiving be made for...kings and all those in authority, that we may live peaceful and quiet lives in all godliness and holiness.

1 TIMOTHY 2:1–2, NIV

the leadership of the United Nations.

Guide me to the current issues and problems You want me to focus prayer on, both in our country and in the world. Just now I especially pray about _____. And I bring to You some current political issues and events that concern me:

_____, _____, _____.

Scripture References (by paragraph)

1. Daniel 4:34–35; Psalm 83:18; Isaiah 40:15, 17; 40:23–24
2. Isaiah 64:4; Luke 18:7–8; Psalm 34:1; 55:17
3. Proverbs 21:1; Psalm 33:10–11; Lamentations 3:37; Isaiah 8:10; Romans 8:28; Philippians 1:12–14

AS YOU HAVE TIME

MAKING HISTORY. "In John's vision of heaven in Revelation 8:3–5, we see that the same censer [the

vessel filled with burning incense] which brings the prayers of believers before God also casts fire upon the earth. Prayers that go up to heaven help make history on earth. Remember today that your prayers go up like incense in God's presence."
Andrew Murray

PRAYING FOR RULERS. "He determines the course of world events; he removes kings and sets others on the throne" (Daniel 2:21, NLT). Meditate on Scripture passages or stories that encourage you to pray with confidence for rulers, for your nation, for international affairs. You may want to begin with one of the following: Exodus 9:15–16; Psalm 33:10–11; 75:6–7; Isaiah 37:21–22, 33–38; Daniel 4:24–37; Hebrews 11:32–34.

Andrew Murray wrote, "What faith in the power of prayer Paul had! He expected a few feeble and despised Christians to influence the mighty Roman emperors, and help secure peace and order! (1 Timothy 2:1–2). Today we can pray with the same conviction that gripped Paul—that prayer is a powerful influence in how God rules the world."

Consider memorizing these words of David Bentley-Taylor:

> The power of prayer cannot be diminished
> by distance; it is not limited by age,
> infirmity, political changes or restrictions.
> The power of prayer in the life of an
> obedient Christian can only be undermined
> by neglect.

PRAY FOR
WORLD EVENTS AND PEACE.

Father, what awful things take place in our
fallen world, where people and nations rebel
against You and Your good purposes. On every hand
I hear of abuse, terrorism, atrocities, massacres,
oppressive regimes, corrupt political systems, and
wars constantly raging throughout the world.

I lift these to You, Lord, for You are the King
of the nations, exalted above all the peoples. I praise
Your great and awesome name, for You nullify the
counsel of the nations, You frustrate the plans of the
peoples. The nations roar like the roaring of many
waters, but in Your time You will rebuke them. You
act, and who can reverse it? And You are able to give
me wisdom as I pray for world events.

May the distressing situations around the world
serve to deepen and refine all who love You and call
on You. In special ways protect them. Bring
deliverance in times of danger, turning aside the

"*He* determines the course of world events."

DANIEL 2:21, NLT

schemes of evil people. And use the traumatic events to turn thousands, even millions, to Christ, as You've been doing in many countries.

I plead with You that, again and again, leaders will make wise decisions and justice will rule. May negotiations between nations and warring factions result in fair treaties that will restore peace.

Most of all, hasten the day when the government of the whole world will be on Christ's shoulders, bringing peace that will never end.

Scripture References (by paragraph)

1. Psalm 2:1–3
2. Revelation 15:3; Psalm 99:2–3; 33:10;
   Isaiah 17:13; 43:13
3. Psalm 27:1–3; 40:1–3; 91:1–4; 107:13–14; 146:9
4. Luke 18:7–8
5. Isaiah 9:6–7

As You Have Time

GOD'S POINT OF VIEW. To pray more effectively, ask God "that you may see things, as it were, from his point of view" (Colossians 1:9, Phillips). Take time to absorb Scriptures that help you see world and personal events as God sees them.

Our God is the Supreme Ruler—the blessed, behind-the-scenes Controller of all things (1 Timothy 6:15, Phillips). Why does this loving and all-powerful God allow the traumatic events we've been praying about? The Bible does not spell out all of His reasons—"How could man ever understand his reasons for action, or explain his methods of working?" (Romans 11:33, Phillips). But it does give insights into how He uses troubles and disasters for good ("Man's extremity is God's opportunity"). And it shows that He looks to us, through prayer, to cause

Him to achieve His good and eternal results.

Consider these Scriptures on God's rule:

"All governments have been placed in power by God.... He decides who will rise and who will fall.... The LORD shatters the plans of the nations and thwarts all their schemes. But the LORD's plans stand firm forever; his intentions can never be shaken.... When the earth quakes and its people live in turmoil, I am the One who keeps its foundations firm." (Romans 13:1; Psalm 75:7; 33:10–11; 75:3, NLT)

PRAY AGAINST SATAN; PRAISE
FOR VICTORY IN CHRIST.

Father in heaven, thank You for including me
as an intercessor, as one who, in Jesus' name,
can help defeat the wicked one. How I rejoice that
Jesus is Victor over all the powers of evil, including
Satan himself.

I praise You that on the cross Jesus stripped the
evil rulers and authorities of their power and won
the victory over them—and that death could not
keep Him in its power. You showed Your
incomparable power by raising Him from the dead
and seating Him in the place of supreme honor at
Your right hand, a place infinitely superior to any
other rule, authority, power, or lordship, both visible
and invisible. There He now reigns in power for
us—and prays for us! So great is His power that His
enemies cringe before Him!

And You have raised me up and seated me with
Him! I am in Him, high above all our spiritual

"*You* will not succeed by your own strength or power, but by My Spirit," says the LORD All-Powerful.

ZECHARIAH 4:6, NCV

enemies; and He is in me, far greater than Satan who is in the world.

Thank You that these things are true of all Your children. We are on the winning side! So I stand boldly before Your throne, grateful that I'm not praying alone. Rather, I'm joining Your Son and all Your "prayer warriors" as we strive in prayer against the enemy—as we advance Your purposes and defeat Satan's purposes in lives and situations throughout the world. And in our lives and situations.

Father, because of this great privilege as Your child, I stand boldly before You and pray for

_____, _____, and _____.

I praise You for the overwhelming victories we win as we pray in the name of Jesus—the Name above all names, both now and in all the ages to come.

Scripture References (by paragraph)

1. Psalm 45:3–4
2. Colossians 2:15; Acts 2:24; Romans 1:4;
   Ephesians 1:19–22; Romans 8:34, Phillips; Psalm 66:3
3. Ephesians 2:6; 1 John 4:4; Ephesians 6:10–12, 18
4. —
5. Romans 8:37; Philippians 2:9–11; Ephesians 1:21

AS YOU HAVE TIME

THE POWERS THAT HINDER. Andrew Murray wrote, "All the powers of evil seek to hinder our prayer life because prayer, by nature, involves conflict with opposing forces. May God give us grace to strive in prayer until we prevail."

To defeat the evil one through prayer, we must take up the shield of faith and the sword of the Spirit—the Word of God. We learn to wield these weapons with great skill as we use statements and truths from the Scriptures in our prayers. This increases our faith and puts the enemy to flight.

(See 2 Chronicles 13:18; Romans 10:17.)

Study Ephesians 6:10–18, the Bible's most complete "call to arms" for spiritual warfare.

OUR POSITION OF TRIUMPH. To further prepare for spiritual battle, feed your soul on Christ's triumph through the Cross (Colossians 2:15), on the surpassing greatness of His power (Ephesians 1:19–22), on your exalted position in Christ (Ephesians 2:6), and on the high privilege of living in union with your risen and reigning Lord (Colossians 3:1–4). As you meditate on these truths, memorize them, and let the Spirit grip your heart with them, you'll be prepared to intercede for those facing spiritual attack or oppression and for spiritual ventures that threaten the enemy.

Satan loves to attack before a venture for Christ and after a victory. Be alert for these times when your prayers are especially needed.

S. D. Gordon wrote:

Prayer is insisting upon Jesus' victory and
the retreat of the enemy on each particular
spot and heart problem concerned.

PRAY THAT GOD'S PEOPLE WILL
REALIZE THEIR WORLDWIDE
CALLING.

Dear Lord, how much You love every person
in the world and hate to see anyone perish!
You are not content for people in vast areas of the
earth to sit in darkness without Your Cross lifted
high. I am grateful that I can work along with You
in Your worldwide purposes.

Thank You that these days of prayer have
helped me pray in new ways for myself and others.
What a privilege to join Christ in His intercession—
to have Him and His Spirit as my nearest and best
prayer partners! How gracious of You to welcome
me into Your innermost circle of love as Father, Son,
and Holy Spirit. And to think that my prayers are
highly significant in Your eyes, and that they can
make a great difference in my life, job, family,
friends, and marriage—and in countless other lives!

May Your Spirit plant Your burden for the
world ever more deeply within me—and within all

$\mathcal{G}$od be gracious to us and bless us, and cause His face to shine upon us—that Thy way may be known on the earth, Thy salvation among all nations.

PSALM 67:1–2

Your children. May He overwhelm us with the privilege of living solely for You and Your kingdom throughout the world so that rival interests will lose their lustre and their hold on us. Help us to realize that "he is no fool who gives what he cannot keep to gain what he cannot lose" (Jim Elliott). Stir us to give, to go, but most of all to pray.

May we hasten the day when Christ will return and the knowledge of You will fill the earth as the waters fill the sea.

COUNT ON GOD'S GRACIOUS WORKING IN YOUR LIFE. "May the God of peace...equip you with everything good for doing his will, and may he work in us what is pleasing to him through Jesus Christ, to whom be glory for ever and ever. Amen."

Scripture References (by paragraph)

1. 2 Peter 3:9; Acts 26:18; 20:24
2. —
3. Matthew 6:33; 2 Timothy 2:3–7; Isaiah 11:9
4. Hebrews 13:20–21, NLT

As You Have Time

RECEIVING THE BENEFITS. Pray that believers will yield to Christ and that His Spirit will take full possession of them; as you pray this, yield yourself anew and count on the Spirit's gracious control and fullness in your own life. Pray that believers will feed richly on God's Word, then pray, "Lord, may I do the same." And as you ask the Lord to remove sins and deficiencies in others, let Him search your heart and reveal your own sins and shortcomings.

Don't miss the opportunity to receive for

yourself the same benefits you ask for others.

OUR WORLDWIDE CALLING. God blessed Abraham so that through his descendants (and, supremely, Jesus Christ) he could be a blessing to the whole world through prayer as well as service. Every believer, as a spiritual descendent of Abraham (Galatians 3:19), is likewise blessed to be part of God's blessing to the whole world.

Murray was deeply burdened that God's people fulfill their calling to bless the entire world through prayer as well as service. He wrote: "If this were preached and believed and practiced, our mission work would be radically changed. Huge numbers of willing intercessors would be added. Cry to God that we His people will realize our world-wide calling."

"This world is God's prodigal son, and He is heartbroken over it" (S. D. Gordon).

An Invitation to Continue

Congratulations! You have completed something far more significant than graduating with highest honors, winning a gold medal in the Olympics, or becoming a Nobel Prize winner. Your praying has brought joy to God and rich blessings to many people.

Besides that, think of the benefits to you. The living God, awesome and glorious beyond imagining, has granted you the honor of joining His beloved Son in His ministry of intercession. And as you have prayed, you've actually been partnering with the Father and the Son and the Holy Spirit. You can't go higher than that!

We encourage you to revisit this prayer venture often. You'll find that the thirty-one-day journey gets better each time. Your warm, abiding relationship with God will grow yet deeper. You and those you pray for will enjoy His love and rich gifts.

You'll help release the Spirit's power in needy places nearby and throughout the world. And in fresh ways you'll find your heart tuned into God's exciting and eternal purposes. All this, plus eternal dividends that will far outweigh your investment. God always sees to it that you receive far more than you give.

WAYS TO GROW IN PRAYER

Prayer can help bring rich and satisfying renewal to our lives. But it's not simply a nice addition we decide to tack onto a lukewarm and stunted spiritual life. Prayer won't grow well by itself.

To benefit fully through prayer, we must plant it in a well-watered garden, where it will grow along with other spiritual attitudes and practices. If any of these are missing, weeds grow up and choke our prayer life, making it more of a burden than a blessing.

The thirty-one days touch on many of the spiritual responses that nurture prayer—and that prayer, in turn, nurtures. For example, yielding to Christ as Lord (day 7), depending on the Holy Spirit (day 11), praising and giving thanks (day 21), and using God's Word in prayer (day 24) all focus on aspects of spiritual growth that work together as we mature in Christ.

In the following pages, we consider more fully eight vital areas of our spiritual life that significantly affect praying. Only as we nurture a growing relationship with the Lord can our prayer life thrive.

1. Cultivate Faith through Pursuing God

Faith is trusting God—counting on Him to be who He says He is and to do what He says He will do. Picture a man who is a tremendous husband—an excellent provider, strong and affectionate, a good listener, eager to help, excellent with the children, honest, and faithful to his wife. Would we be surprised if his wife trusted him? Of course not. Rather, we'd be amazed if she didn't.

We're often amazed when we meet someone who has a deep faith in God. But God is stronger, more loving, more eager to help, more faithful, and infinitely more wonderful than the best husband in the world. Why don't we trust Him more? Because we don't know Him well. Perhaps we haven't put Him to the test through obedience and prayer, and then watched Him keep His word. We're left to suffer from not knowing Him and from the resulting misconceptions that strangle our faith.

But we can change this. We can study the Scriptures day by day with the earnest prayer, "Lord, show me what You are like. By Your Spirit impress truths about You on my heart. Use Your Word to clear out my wrong ideas and to plant deep in my heart a true knowledge of You."

For years as a couple we've made a rewarding pastime of collecting Bible verses about God. What treasures we have come across thus far! And we've only just begun. We search out and savor passages that tell us about God's holiness, His supreme majesty and perfect purity, His righteousness, His truthfulness. We've learned more about how wise He is, how loving, how powerful, how worthy of our trust.

Our goal is to understand God better and value Him more. We meditate on the passages, seeking to let the Holy Spirit grip our hearts with them. Why not join us? Record your discoveries. Perhaps start a notebook where you can write down exciting truths about God for years to come.

Your faith will flourish as you focus on God and praise Him for how awesome and wonderful He is. You might want to begin with the following passages: Exodus 15:6–7, 11; Deuteronomy 32:4; 1 Chronicles 29:11–13; Jeremiah 10:6–7, 12; 31:3; 32:17, 27; Lamentations 3:22–23; Daniel 4:35; Zephaniah 3:17; Revelation 15:3–4.

Ask the Lord for a growing thirst for Him. Pray often about this, for yourself and for others. Begin with A. W. Tozer's prayer from *The Pursuit of God:*

> O God, I have tasted Your goodness, and it has both satisfied me and made me thirsty for more.... O God, the Triune God, I want to want You; I long to be filled with longing.... Show me Your glory, I pray, so that I may know You indeed.... Give me grace to rise and follow You up from this misty lowland where I have wandered so long. In Jesus' name, Amen.

2. Count on the Truth of Instant Forgiveness

When we sense we are living in obedience to God, it's easier to pray with confidence. But what about the times when we haven't been trusting and obeying the Lord? Or the times when we think, *I've confessed my sin, yet my conscience still bothers me—and my confidence is still shattered?* In times like that, we tend to avoid prayer, or we come before God like a puppy with its tail between its legs.

How can we regain our confidence?

First of all, be assured that the Lord is always eager to forgive and cleanse you. He longs for you to confess your sins, including your lack of trust, and to reaffirm your commitment to Christ as your Lord. Think of confession as part of maintaining a healthy relationship with God and an essential part of your obedience. Another part of your obedience is to count on the fact that the Lord has kept His promise to forgive you and immediately relates to you just as if you had never sinned!

A powerful Scripture that can help you grow in this area is 1 John 1:9: "If we confess our sins, he is faithful and just and will forgive us our sins and purify us from all unrighteousness" (NIV). Other key passages are Psalm 32:5; Proverbs 28:13; Psalm 130:3–4; and Romans 4:7–8.

Immediately after you confess, you can pray with boldness before God! When you forget this and get trapped in self-condemnation, be encouraged by the response of the devout Frances of Sales, sixteenth-century Bishop of Geneva: "Well my poor soul, here we are in the ditch again, in spite of our earnest resolve to stay out of it. Ah well, let us get out and go on our way, and we'll do well enough, God helping us."

Don't let vague guilt hinder your prayers. Satan likes to attack us with a general, condemning, accusing sense of sinfulness and failure—that's why he is described as "the accuser of our brothers" (Revelation 12:10, NIV). In contrast, when the Holy Spirit convicts us of sin He is specific. He is firm and persistent but also gentle. He's not out to condemn us but to liberate us and draw us back into fellowship with God.

If you find yourself oppressed by a thick cloud of vague guilt, remember that God is not in the business of condemning His children. That's the devil's business. So choose to resist him. Thank the Father that Satan is a defeated enemy, that Jesus is Victor over him, and that you need not be taken in by his oppression and lies. Thank the Father that His Son bore all your guilt on the cross and that now your true self is clean and righteous. Praise Him that He does not treat you as your sins deserve, for His love and mercy are as high as the heavens are above the earth. Then go on with your interceding, asking the Holy Spirit to show you clearly if there's any specific sin He wants you to confess.

After we confess our sin, we should resist any urge to scold or punish ourselves. This is our self-centered, worldly way of trying to buy forgiveness or reform ourselves. The pathway back to obedience is seeing ourselves as forgiven and cleansed and able to conquer sin by Christ's holy and powerful life within us.

Other passages that may help you are Romans 8:1; 2 Corinthians 5:21; Isaiah 53:4–5; Revelation 12:10–11; Colossians 2:13–15; and Psalm 103:10–13.

3. ABIDE IN CHRIST

Hudson Taylor, a great missionary to China during the 1800s, had been groping through a period of dense darkness. He felt overwhelmed by his failures and inadequacy and lack of power. He knew that all he needed was in Christ—but the big question he wrestled with was how to get it out of Christ and into himself.

Then, through a letter from a coworker, the Lord opened Taylor's eyes to see that he was so united to Christ that he shared His life. He was simply to accept Christ's invitation to "abide in Me" and not try to get anything out of Him. He wrote his sister:

> How great seemed my mistake in wishing to get the sap, the fullness out of Him!... The vine is not the root merely, but all— root, stem, branches, twigs.... And Jesus is

not that alone—He is oil and sunshine, air
and showers, and ten thousand times
more than we have ever dreamed, wished
for, or needed. Oh, the joy of seeing this
truth! Can Christ be rich and I poor? Can
your head be well fed while your body
starves?

"Abide in Me"—what an incredible invitation!
Jesus (think of who He is!) wants an intimate
relationship with us, a relationship of mutual
enjoyment, with us living in Him and He in us.
Abiding in Christ means to depend on Him,
enjoying our spiritual union with Him and allowing
Him to meet our needs.

"Abiding" is a basic preparation for praying the
way God wants us to pray. Think of the promise in
John 15:7, "If you abide in Me, and My words abide
in you, ask whatever you wish, and it shall be done
for you." As your hand experiences the life of your
body as its own, so as you abide in Christ you
experience the life of Christ as your own. Life that is
fresh, pure, joyous, fruitful, free of anxiety, and full of

faith. Life that is wrapped up in the desires that are on God's heart. Then when you pray, you express His longings; you want what He wants. And so He does what you ask.

Abiding is not complicated or strenuous. It's as simple as the new birth. The Holy Spirit did His quiet work within us, making us ready to trust Christ. Then we acknowledged our need. We turned from depending on our own works and worthiness, and yielded to Christ as the one source of forgiveness and eternal life. We trusted in Him as our Lord and Savior with no conscious reservations. The scenario and feelings were different for each of us. But two things were the same: the turning and the trusting.

Abiding in Christ is much the same, except that it requires God's continual working, not His once-for-all work. We are "in Christ"—we don't have to try to get there; and the words "in Christ" could be translated "in union with Christ." We simply agree to a constant dependence on Him. We turn, time and again, from our own abilities, our

We enjoy Andrew Murray's description of abiding: "Abiding in Jesus is nothing but the giving up of oneself to be ruled and taught and led, and so resting in the arms of Everlasting Love."

Years after Hudson Taylor learned the secret of abiding in Christ, someone asked him if he was always conscious of abiding in Christ. He replied, "While sleeping last night, did I cease to abide in your home because I was unconscious of the fact? We should never be conscious of not abiding in Christ."

What a difference it makes in our praying when we abide in Christ!

4. WALK HUMBLY WITH YOUR GOD

If we want God to work in us and for us, answering our prayers, then humility is not merely a nice extra. It's indispensable. "God opposes the proud but gives grace to the humble.... Blessed are the destitute and helpless in the realm of the spirit, for theirs is the kingdom of heaven" (James 4:6; Matthew 5:3, Wuest). No wonder one of the major things God requires of us is to walk humbly with our God (Micah 6:8). If we don't, God will oppose us. We cannot pray as the Lord desires if we're not aware of our true neediness.

Humility has nothing to do with being weak or pessimistic. It's simply thinking about God and ourselves realistically. As we choose humility, God gives us special grace to pray in ways that please Him.

How often we slip into self-sufficiency, leaning on our natural wisdom and abilities, our own power and forcefulness, our own whatever. That's pride. But it can just as easily be pride when we bemoan our weaknesses or lack of natural abilities. You see, either way we're caught in human values that measure us by our abilities and personality rather than by God's evaluation.

What is true humility? Think of it as a two-sided coin. On the one side, genuine humility accepts Jesus' pronouncement, "Without Me you can do nothing" (John 15:5, NKJV). On the other side of the same reality, genuine humility declares with glad confidence, "I have strength for all things in Christ Who empowers me [I am ready for anything and equal to anything through Him Who infuses inner strength into me]" (John 15:5; Philippians 4:13, AMP).

Humility says, like the cherished hymn, "I need You. Oh, I need You!" Then it lets faith take over with the glad affirmation: "I have You! Oh, I have You!" Far more than we know, we are needy persons. Yet we're fully supplied persons as we humbly trust in Him.

In ourselves, by our own abilities and wisdom, we are completely unable to do anything that pleases God. Knowing this prepares us to yield to Christ and trust Him as our life and our sufficiency. Most of us require frequent reminders of our needs and failures; these prod us into humbling ourselves enough to trust God. Sometimes we need the rug pulled out from under us. We have to fall on our faces so that the truth of our total need for God becomes more than just words. This point of personal poverty is a place of profit; there the wonder of abiding in Christ and the relief of living by His life can begin to dawn in our hearts. Only then can we begin to live and love and pray as He desires. Only then can we take hold of His strength and experience His grace in abundance.

Our failures and unmet needs are in reality great blessings in disguise. They remind us that we're not qualified to run our own lives. They press us to commit ourselves to Christ and trust in Him. They keep us humble. And humility is the only realistic way that we, mere humans, can relate to our supreme and holy God. So make it a practice to bow often before the Lord with a repentant, humble spirit (Isaiah 57:15).

Why does God hate pride? Because it's an empty lie. It's a false confidence that blocks His children's connection with the only solution to their deepest needs. And pride brings immense loss to God because it deprives Him of the genuine intimacy with us that He longs for.

There's no other way to walk with God but to walk humbly. And, as we humble ourselves and honor God, we qualify for the promise, "Those who

honor Me I will honor" (1 Samuel 2:30). He will
honor us, and He will also honor our prayers.

5. DEPEND ON THE WORD, NOT FEELINGS

Do you feel at times that your prayers just seem to
bounce off the ceiling? Nearly everyone does. Even
people who are walking with God with no
unconfessed sin in their lives experience this.
Sometimes they feel their prayers are really "getting
through"; at other times they feel their words are
going nowhere. Are such feelings an indicator of
how God views our prayers?

We get in trouble when we depend on our
feelings in prayer. We start thinking we have to be in
a praying mood to pray, or we call our petitions
"good prayers" if they give us a certain feeling. It's
much better to just decide to pray as God
commands—regardless of how we feel. Charles
Spurgeon wrote, "We should pray when we are in a
praying mood, for it would be sinful to neglect so
fair an opportunity. We should pray when we are
not in a praying mood because it would be

dangerous to remain in so unhealthy a condition."

It's not that feelings are out of place. Many people, in Bible times and since, have prayed with a deep sense of distress or urgency. The afflicted man in Psalm 102 prayed with loud groaning, "My heart is blighted and withered like grass.... I am like a desert owl, like an owl among the ruins." If we have deep troubles, God tells us to pour out our hearts to Him (Psalm 62:8). If He gives us intense concern for others, we're to pray with intense feelings. If He makes us particularly conscious of His presence, let's enjoy it. And if the Spirit carries us along in prayer, let's be grateful. But if not, we can still pray, depending on the Word, like the jet pilot who depends on what the instruments say rather than how he feels. We can't judge the success of our prayers by our emotions. And we're not to let our emotions determine whether or not we pray.

Leaving our feelings in God's hands helps us be more consistent in prayer. If we find ourselves floundering, we can ask the Lord to give us insight as we conduct a "heart checkup":

* Am I yielding to Christ's lordship and abiding in Him?
* Have I confessed every known sin?
* Am I praying in Jesus' name—in His merits and not my own?
* Am I praying in agreement with what I understand to be God's will and purposes?
* Am I praying in faith based on God's Word?

If these checkup questions show that our hearts are right, we can depend on God's promises to hear and answer us. He says in Jeremiah 33:3, "Call to Me, and I will answer you." We can pray "in the Spirit," directed and helped by Him, and depending on the Word He inspired—no matter how we feel.

Christians vary greatly in how they generally feel when they pray. Some have intense emotions; others are more subdued. Resist the urge to compare your feelings in prayer with how others pray. God has made you unique. How you pray— and how you feel as you pray—will also be unique to you and special to God.

Remember that fluctuating emotions are a

normal part of being human. Our physical lives move in cycles that affect our emotions, with peaks of high energy and troughs of low energy. So when God seems to have disappeared as far as your feelings go, you honor Him in a unique way when you pray anyway.

If you are troubled about an overall lack of positive emotions during prayer, bring your concern to God. Ask Him to overcome any patterns of living or thinking that may be hindering you. But don't get trapped in the error of our feelings-centered age. Feelings are not the only authentic part of our inner person. And being honest in the scriptural sense does not mean expressing all our feelings or responding to all our emotional impulses and preferences. We also have a mind and a will. We can turn our minds to God's commands and with our will choose to obey, even when our feelings don't cooperate. We please God when we choose to let Him and His Word, rather than feelings, govern us.

Hudson Taylor received amazing answers to prayer. Someone asked him late in life if he always felt joyful when he prayed. He replied that his heart usually felt like wood when he prayed and that most of his major victories came through "emotionless prayer."

Yet our emotions matter greatly to God, and He doesn't ask us to ignore them. When your emotions are unpleasant or absent, don't equate this with sin. Jesus Himself expressed troubled emotions in His prayer life. So tell God how you feel and give your emotions to Him. Then choose to bring Him joy by letting Him, not your feelings, govern your prayer choices.

6. Learn to Be Still before God

How can we prepare our hearts for prayer? By cultivating a quiet heart before the Lord, both in our times alone with Him and throughout our days. By letting Him lead us beside still waters.

Moses wrote in Deuteronomy 4:39, "Acknowledge and take to heart this day that the LORD is God in heaven above and on the earth below" (NIV). We're to think about the truths God has revealed about Himself, poring over them attentively. Then we're to pause and be still—relax, let go, cease striving—and know in the depths of our being that this awesome, exalted, dependable person is God (Psalm 46:10). We can let our thoughts about His greatness lead us to an inner stillness that absorbs His reality and responds to Him with relaxed confidence.

"In returning and rest you shall be saved; in quietness and confidence shall be your strength" we read in Isaiah 30:15 (NKJV). Then at the end of chapter 40, Isaiah tells us that those who wait expectantly on the Lord will renew their strength. Waiting on God and resting in Him have much in common. Both result in absorbing His strength; both involve truly tuning in to God and His Word. The more we have His Word dwelling richly in our hearts, the more it can help us be quiet, restful, and attentive to Him during all our waking hours.

Prayer is conversation, not just monologue. We're to listen as well as speak. God's voice is often "still" and "small" and we can easily drown it out. By waiting in quietness before Him, we express our respect and adoration, and we let Him speak to our hearts. He may speak through a sense of His nearness, His love, His welcome, His power, His guidance. He may bring to mind Scriptures that speak to our need.

The strength we absorb from the Lord and the quietness of heart He gives prepare us to pray effectively. We're able to come before God with an alive expectancy rather than wearily dragging ourselves into His presence—though dragging ourselves wearily into His presence is a good thing to do when necessary! But it will be necessary less often as we let God drain away our inner stress and infuse us with His strength day by day.

7. Pray with a Nonjudgmental Attitude

When we intercede without love, we pray without power—we are "only a resounding gong or a clanging cymbal" (1 Corinthians 13:1, NIV). And a common form of lovelessness is a judgmental spirit. How easily, even when we pray with deep concern for others, we can allow a critical attitude to creep in.

John Hyde, a missionary to India so noted for his prayer life that he was called Praying Hyde, became burdened to pray for an Indian pastor. Thinking of the pastor's coldness and the resulting deadness of his church, Hyde began to pray: "O Father, You know how cold..." Before he could finish the sentence, the words came to mind, "He who touches him, touches the apple of My eye" (see Zechariah 2:8). Hyde cried out for God to forgive him for being, like Satan, an accuser of a believer—even in prayer.

Hyde decided to turn his thoughts from the negatives that were temporarily true in his fellow servant to the things that were both true and admirable. He asked God to show him all that deserved praise in the pastor's life. Much came to mind, and Hyde spent his prayer time thanking and praising God for his Indian brother. Shortly afterward he learned that, at the very time he was praising and giving thanks, his brother in Christ experienced spiritual renewal. The pastor's life and preaching took on new power.

Sin is fleeting in the lives of God's children. It won't last forever. It is not part of our new nature. In Christ we are cleansed and complete, and God has committed Himself to finish the good work He has begun in us. We can pray for each other's spiritual needs, asking God to deliver. But especially when we're asking God to overcome negative qualities, we must be on guard against the sin of a critical, proud spirit cloaked in prayer.

Have you noticed that Paul's recorded prayers for believers—even those who needed correction—were filled not with negative requests but with thanksgiving and positive requests, with the things he wanted to see in their lives? In Philippians 1:9 he did not say, "I pray you'll get over your quarreling," but "I pray that your love for each other will overflow more and more." (See also Ephesians 3:16–19; Philippians 1:9–11; Colossians 1:9–12; and 1 Corinthians 1:4–8.) When we're concerned about a person's negative qualities, it helps to think through to the corresponding positive qualities we hope for, and pray for those. We personally find it easier to have faith for the positives than against the negatives.

8. View Prayer As a Way of Life

The habit of quietly tuning in to God helps us obey His command, "Pray continually," or "Keep on praying" (1 Thessalonians 5:17 NIV, NLT). How can we pray all the time when so many things demand our attention? What does this command really mean?

Could it mean that, apart from our times set apart for prayer, much of our praying is a simple awareness of the Lord, with an attitude of dependence or gratitude, with a quiet, almost wordless sense of communion? This God-centered attitude is an outgrowth of our abiding in Christ. It prepares us to bring requests to the Lord as they come to mind throughout the day, for both tiny and giant things. In other words, we include our best, our heavenly Friend, in our daily experiences rather than just ignoring Him. Sometimes we sort of mumble casual remarks or a simple "Yes, Lord" that acknowledges His presence. At other times we voice a "Thank You" or a quiet "Hallelujah." Sometimes we share with Him an ongoing conversation about our thoughts and feelings, our concerns and desires.

As we abide in Christ, our minds are like the hand of a scale that points upward unless something is being weighed. In a similar way, our thoughts can be aware of the Lord, with an upward focus, except when something needs our full attention—some task, some social interaction. Even then we can now and then direct quick "arrow" prayers to the Lord about what we are doing—sometimes just a glance of our mind His way that says, "I need help."

When the need for immediate focus on the task at hand passes, turning our fuller attention to the Lord is again possible. We can once more lift to Him our love, as well as our needs, reminding Him that we're depending on Him. This means we'll be available to intercede whenever the Lord brings to mind some person or need or situation, near or far.

Don't most of us need to pray more constantly? This suggests an important "change me" request.

Pray (now and often) that the Lord will help you turn your heart to Him more frequently throughout the day and that this will develop into praying continually. Ask Him to overcome anything in you that hinders a constant, quiet, prayerful spirit—anything that divides your heart or diverts you from communion with your Lord.

Also pray that you will turn to God more often with short arrow prayers—prayers that rise to God throughout your waking hours for people you see, people you relate to, and people who come to mind. Does someone remind you of a friend? Does the news tell of people in need? Use these daily promptings to release quick, on-the-spot prayers.

I cannot tell why there should come to me
A thought of someone miles and years away,
In swift insistence on the memory,
Unless there is a need that I should pray.
Perhaps just then my friend has fiercer fight,
A more appalling weakness, a decay
Of courage, darkness, some lost sense of right;
And so, in case he needs my prayers I pray.

ROSALIND GOFORTH

While on earth Jesus prayed continually. Before feeding the five thousand, at the raising of Lazarus, before choosing His disciples, with His disciples, for His disciples, all night, early in the morning, in the garden, on the cross—Jesus prayed. Prayer was a way of life to Him and still is today as He continually intercedes for us.

Prayer will become a more constant, more treasured part of our lives, too, as we become more like the Lord.

BIBLIOGRAPHY

References are listed in the order they first appear in each section of the book.

PART ONE

Gordon, S. D. *Quiet Talks on Prayer.* New York: Grosset & Dunlap, 1904.

PART TWO

Murray, Andrew. *The Ministry of Intercession in The Andrew Murray Collection.* Uhrichsville, Ohio: Barbour and Company, Inc., 1995.

The Unknown Christian, The Kneeling Christian. Grand Rapids: Zondervan Publishing House, 1986.

Goforth, Rosalind. *Goforth of China.* Grand Rapids: Zondervan Publishing House, 1937.

Mueller, George. *An Hour with George Mueller.* Chicago: Moody Press, 1944.

Daily Meditations for Prayer. Grand Rapids: Baker Book House Company, 1978.

Elliott, Elizabeth. *Shadow of the Almighty.* New York: Harper and Brothers, 1958.

Pierson, Arthur T. *George Mueller of Bristol.* New York: Loizeaux Brothers, Inc., 1899.

Gurnall, William. *The Christian in Complete Armor.* Glasgow, Scotland: 1662.

Taylor, Dr. and Mrs. Howard. *Hudson Taylor's Spiritual Secret.* London, England: China Inland Mission, 1935.

Myers, Warren and Ruth. *Praise: A Door to God's Presence.* Colorado Springs: NavPress, 1987.

Murray, Andrew. *With Christ in the School of Prayer* in
The Andrew Murray Collection. Uhrichsville, Ohio:
Barbour and Company, Inc., 1995.

Gordon, S. D. *Quiet Talks on Prayer*. New York:
Grosset & Dunlap, 1904.

Gordon, S. D. *Quiet Talks on Power*. Grand Rapids:
Baker Book House Company, 1903.

PART THREE

Tozer, A. W. *The Pursuit of God*. Harrisburg, Penn.:
Christian Publishing, Inc., 1948.

Taylor, Dr. and Mrs. Howard. *Hudson Taylor's Spiritual
Secret*. London, England: China Inland Mission,
1935.

Murray, Andrew. *Abide in Christ*. New York: Grosset
& Dunlap, 1904.

Eastman, Dick. *Change the World School of Prayer.* World Literature Crusade, n.d.

Goforth, Rosalind. *Goforth of China.* Grand Rapids: Zondervan Publishing House, 1937.

Offering Free Resources
of *hope* & *encouragement*